SIMPLE • POWERFUL • M

Dancing
ON THE RUBBLE

The Essence of Living

Includes the
Study Guide
and access
to online
Supplimental
Material

ROY H. CANTRELL Ph.D.

outskirts
press

"You have turned for me my mourning into dancing;
You have put off my sackcloth and clothed me with gladness."
Psalm 30:11

"Rejoice in that day and leap for joy!"
Luke 6:23

"Hope shouts loudest from the top of the rubble."
Roy H. Cantrell

"Nothing changes until something moves."
--Albert Einstein

To: —————————————————————

From: _____

Author Roy H. Cantrell, his wife Kaye, and Sophie.
Photo by Karen Marks

Roy H. Cantrell
Phil. 1:3-11

I have known and admired Roy Cantrell for over forty years. Through all that life has thrown at him and his family, I have always known him to be a man after God's own heart. *Dancing on the Rubble* is a testament to Dr. Cantrell's trust in and reliance on a faithful, healing, loving, and redeeming God who has, in turn, empowered him to serve as a witness to and servant of Jesus Christ. Dr. Cantrell has walked the walk, and you will find sage guidance between the covers of *Dancing on the Rubble* that will enable you to live in freedom, hope, peace, and above all love, through the power of the Holy Spirit.

Ed George, MTS, ACPE Certified Educator, BCC

This book is a must-read for every believer, but especially for those who struggle with living free. Dr. Cantrell nudges our inner selves to wake up and rise above the rubble in our lives. We can be free to "dance" if we are willing to see the rubble as an opportunity instead of an obstacle. This book will be helpful on an individual or small group study basis. It's not a one-time read; it is a book for your library, a book you will find yourself reaching for often.

Betty Rushford, M.Th, D. Min

Dr. Roy Cantrell puts life into practical perspective in this book. If you want to know how to get the most meaning in your "darkest hour," this book is a must read. God never intended that we go through an experience and get nothing out of it. *Dancing on the Rubble* provides us with ways to see the light of Christ even when we feel overwhelmed by the dark times in our lives. So, know that whatever contributes to the heap of rubble that we experience, this book shows us how to overcome the rubbish heap and be free of it. May God speak to you as you read this book.

Dr. Isaac O. Obure
Founder, Future Life Tabernacle
Siaya, Kenya, Africa

By focusing on our salvation through Jesus Christ, Dr. Cantrell teaches us how we can dance on top of the rubble that exists in all our lives. We will learn some "dance steps" when reading this book. Then we will feel free to "dance."

Joe Haskins, MD

My friend, Dr. Roy Cantrell has penned a much-needed work. As he has pointed out, dancing on the rubble is "the essence of living, Christians, too, encounter problems, tragedies, hurts, and even unjustified accusations. It is not often that the kind of help this book offers is available. Dr. Cantrell not only identifies the problems well, but he also provides the necessary and welcomed responses to the tragic situations that arise in life. Keep in mind as you read that this book is pointing you to the answer for which you are looking. Choose that answer and you, too, will be "dancing on the rubble."

Len Showalter
President, Len Ministries
Jacksonville, FL

The church today needs a radical change to be empowered to endure the biblical prediction of violence and hatred directed toward everyone, including Christians, in the last days. Dr. Roy Cantrell writes from a heart full of God's love, desiring that God's people live joyfully and free in the Holy Spirit. His third book, *Dancing on the Rubble*, takes us on a God-focused seven step journey from "keep on living" through the pain of life to "keep letting go" where he encourages us to be true to ourselves as we encounter the rubble in our lives. I find this book to be extraordinary, encouraging, and challenging as it penetrates our hidden secrets, helping us to walk in the light as we allow God's Word and the Holy Spirit to guide us to freedom. This book is for every Christian. Two things are required of the reader: humility and the desire to be free.

Samuel Said, PhD

Dr. Cantrell is an Encourager! We have witnessed his ability to minister to individuals in the depths of struggles and despair and turn their most difficult experiences into triumphant and joyous hope. *Dancing on the Rubble* highlights his ability to use the Word of God to turn reader's minds away from the negative experiences that life throws at Christians and focuses on how God restores joy to help them face those issues head on.

Nancy and Terry Womack

A brief review is certainly not going to do justice to the depth of human experience expressed in the pages of this book. The reader will find ways to deal with life issues that become the "rocks" that contribute to the pile of rubble in our lives. Dr. Cantrell's unique presentation of the problems facing Christians is a vital and pertinent message. He provides sound scripture-based solutions for overcoming life's challenges and living joyously in Christ. Dr. Cantrell's insight and understanding of the seven life challenges in *Dancing on the Rubble* speaks to the reader in powerful ways.

Vernon Van Deventer

Whatever heartaches life has dealt us, this book teaches us how to "dance on the rubble" of these dark and faith-threatening events. Inside these pages, readers will learn how to conquer resentment, blame, shame, hatred, depression, unforgiveness, etc. "Casting down imaginations and every high thing that exalts itself against the knowledge of God and bringing into captivity every thought to the obedience of Christ." (II Corinthians 10:5) When ". . . we gird up the loins of our mind [and *Dancing on the Rubble* tells us how]. . .there is hope to the end for the grace . . . of Jesus Christ." (I Peter 1:13 paraphrased)

Larry and Colleen Womack

Through life there are often times of reflection; we experience events and meet people who impact us in different ways. For the many years that I have known him, Roy Cantrell continues to enlighten me with his knowledge and experience. In *Dancing on the Rubble,* a work that is both inspiring and enlightening, Dr. Cantrell continues to cause me to pause, reflect, and consider my ways with God. This book not only provides the reader insight into seven challenges we face throughout our lives, it also provides us with the knowledge needed to overcome them. *Dancing on the Rubble* is sure to enlighten you as it has me.

Gail Stathis, Executive Director
EMG Ministries
Founding Pastor
Glyfada Christian Center, Greece

Dancing on the Ruble will lift up the despondent and encourage the dejected. And it will also remind those who lift up others and those who encourage others to be intentional about their walk with the Lord. Pastor Cantrell focuses on key scriptures throughout his inspiring book which pinpoint the difficulties believers face in their journey through life, and then uses those same scriptures to call us back into a sweeter and more meaningful relationship with our Lord and Savior Jesus Christ. This book is from the heart of a pastor. His wisdom and years of experience are poured into the counsel presented in these pages.

Gary Glover
Author, missionary, graphic designer

I have known Roy Cantrell for nearly 40 years. He trained me in personal evangelism and then served as my District Pastor. He was the first person to encourage me to further my formal education and to study, even though I was at a small church and a recession was in full swing. In other words, he wanted me to dance on the rubble or whatever else life threw at me. Roy has exemplified a positive attitude throughout his life, and this book is something that he has lived. If you are depressed or discouraged, this book may be just what you need! Read and enjoy.

Dr. Tim McCaleb

If you read only one book this year, make it this one. It's that encouraging. I have known Roy Cantrell for more than fifty-seven years and have watched his faithfulness through all kinds of circumstances. He writes this book from the overflow of a life that has learned to "dance on the rubble."

Terry Mahan
Founding Pastor
The Father's House Church
Leesburg, FL

Roy Cantrell's new book is a powerful reminder that God will never leave or forsake us. If we look through the eyes of the Holy Spirit, there is a revelation in our rubble. *Dancing on the Rubble* is one of the most encouraging books I have read.

Dennis Daniels
Founder and lead pastor
Grace Community Church

It is with great delight that I can recommend Roy Cantrell and his newest book *Dancing on the Rubble*. I have known Roy, his wife Kaye and family for over 50 Years. I am blessed to have been able to sit under his leadership and ministry at different times in my life. I consider him a close friend and mentor. He has had an amazing journey, has filled various positions in the ministry, but has always remained genuine and authentic. Roy loves God and His Word, and at times it has cost him, but has kept his integrity. Proverbs 23:23a states, "Buy the truth and do not sell it." He loves people and is loved by many. Roy has impacted several generations in the years I have known him and will continue to do so. He speaks from his heart and the experience of his long and fruitful ministry. I can highly recommend this book and I know it will address issues that Christians and Ministers of the Gospel will forever find useful.

Johnny Scroggins
Ministers Fellowship International (MFI)
Australasia Director

Sometimes wisdom is simple. Not simply earned, but simply delivered. Roy Cantrell has an ability to deliver that wisdom with grace, as he has done in this book. I have watched from near and far as he has traveled the journey delivered here, a gift to those of us with ears to hear. I encourage you to learn, or learn again, to live life "dancing on the rubble."

Brian van Deventer
General Director
EME Ministries, Greece

Dedication

To my wife **Ina Kaye** for her enduring love.
To our children **Howie and Karen** for their endless support. .
To our grandchildren who light up my life:
Jonathan, **Christina**, **Cody**, **Trey**, and **Travis**.
To our great grandchildren who bring joy to my world:
McKenzie, Nolan, Reilly, Jenson, Jaden, Zane, Sterling, Luke,
and **Lucas.**
To my sister **Novella** and our great niece **Keagan Kennedy**:
for their constant inspiration; despite disabilities they
are still dancing on their rubble!
And last, but not least, Tony and Ann Jett's son,
Matthew, who is now dancing on the golden streets of heaven.

And to all those who are facing similar challenges of life, or worse, we pray for you that the peace of God may be upon you right now, and that somehow you will grasp hold of the "mustard seed faith" (big enough to move mountains) that God has given you, (Hebrews 10:38; Matthew 17:20; Hebrews 11:6), and declare victory in the name of the Father, Son and Holy Spirit. Hallelujah!

I will survive this!
I will come through this!
This will not destroy me!

Never let a stumble in the road be the end of your journey.
If you do stumble, make it a part of the dance.

Acknowledgements

Great sacrifice and numerous hours of sweat, blood, and tears have gone into this book. I must thank my wife Kaye, who shared in my struggle with Parkinson's to write this book. Her patience and constant encouragement to keep writing despite the many days I was shut away from her in my office.

Our friend Bonnie Lind has spent countless hours editing and proofreading the manuscript, and she has had great patience with my many rewrites. I couldn't have done the book without her. Thank you, Joyce Calfee and Frank Shroyer for your time and proofreading expertise.

Thanks go to Gary Glover and April Mooneyham for designing the cover.

Christian Taylor, thank you for assistance as technological consultant for getting the supplemental materials online at **dancingontherubble.com.**

Thanks also is due all those who took the time to read the manuscript and give an endorsement. Thanks to others who also proofread the manuscript. Thanks to Rebecca Haskins and her lady's prayer group for daily praying for me. I am thankful to Vernon Van Deventer for his prayers and loyal friendship.

I would also like to thank the many people who had a hand in making this book better: our church support group, Robert and Karen Horne, Joseph and Evelyn Bathe, Jack and Loretta Wright, my sisters, Zetta Stein and Novella Brewer; Steve Freeman, Isaac Obure, (in Kenya, Africa), and Tony Belk for promoting my books. Thanks to everyone who shared their personal stories to make this book a special blessing.

I thank my Heavenly Father, His Son, and the Holy Spirit for giving me the strength and guidance and the means to pour myself into this book. I pray every day that *Dancing on the Rubble* will be carried on the wings of the Holy Spirit to empower those who are surrounded by life's rubble to find the courage to rise up and stand then dance on it, all to the glory of Almighty God. Hallelujah!

Foreword

My husband and I have had the privilege of knowing Dr. Roy Cantrell and his family for over fifty years. We've watched him face adversity time and time again. He knows first-hand what it is to face walls of opposition, heartache, and rejection to name only a few of life's issues. With each trial I have seen his faith in God become unshakeable. I've observed his humility and watched his character develop when it looked as though life's battles were going to take him down.

I recall years ago; my husband and I decided to take dancing lessons at a dance studio. The first time we walked out onto the floor, we felt awkward and we were left feeling very insecure. We were introduced to many different dances. How we danced depended on the type of music our instructor chose. By the time we finished our last lesson, we no longer felt awkward. We walked out onto the dance floor with our hearts full of confidence and our heads high. We had learned how to dance.

God has an abundance of music from which to choose. This book and study guide will do for you, the reader, what it has done for others. Dr. Cantrell will be your instructor, and he is immensely qualified to teach you how to dance on each pile of rubble that God allows to come your way. How do I know he is qualified? Because God has been his instructor for a very long time. So, let's get out on the floor together and dance, letting God the Father take the lead to "dance on the rubble."

Loretta and Jack Wright
Christian ministries, retired

Dancing on the Rubble
The Essence of Living

The essence of living is putting God first in one's life. He must be the center of everything because He is the lifeblood that makes it possible to resist the downward pull of the negative forces in one's life. It must be one's goal to always put God at the front of the battle and push upward to rise above the rubble (ruins) and dance on it in celebration of a victorious and larger life.

Rubble is a part of life; you can't avoid it. However, you can, in most cases, rise above the situation and be victorious. Some will live among the rubble, and there are those who will, by God's help, rise above it and cope, no matter how bad things are. You can dance on the rubble even in a horizontal position, spiritually speaking. In fact, some of the greatest testimonies come from those who, by no fault of their own, suffered a tragedy and are physically lying on their backs giving praise to God. Yet, despite everything, they are able to dance on the rubble by the grace of God.

Joni Eareckson Tada is one of the best examples I know as one who sees and practices this gift of grace. She summed up life this way: "Life becomes inspiring not in spite of the problems and the hard hits, but because of them. My goal is to see the world's one billion people with disabilities embraced and encouraged by the church."[1]

Definition of **essence**: Basic, bottom line, core, fundamental, principle, quality, substance. Also: foundation, essentials, key (s), keystone, principle elements, sum and substance. c. 1400 from Anglo-Norman *rabel*. Bits of broken stone probably related to rubbish. Synonyms: ruins, fragments, shards, garbage, remnants, litter.

There is no way that you can go through this study and come out with less faith.

Howie Cantrell
Online Instructor

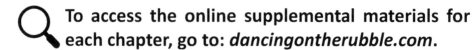

To access the online supplemental materials for each chapter, go to: *dancingontherubble.com*.

Contents

In Everything

Roy H. Cantrell

"In everything give thanks"
is what the Bible says, but
that doesn't sound just right.
How can I say, "thank you, God"
when I'm in serious pain all night?

How can I say, "thank you, God,"
when my marriage is gone
and my heart is broken?
And the children are crying
Because they don't have a home.

How can I say, "thank you, God,"
when my loved one was killed
in a terrible accident today?
To thank You for such a tragedy
sounds like an awful thing to say.

"Dearly beloved," I didn't say
FOR everything be thankful.
I said IN everything give thanks.
Because IN EVERYTHING you face,
I will be there with abundant grace.

Introduction

Dancing on the Rubble is a book we need today. Our nation and our world are going through radical changes as never before. More than 69,029 overdose deaths were recorded in one year. The drug fentanyl was cited as largely responsible for those deaths.[2] The very moral fabric of American's foundation is being shaken with the scourge of opioid addiction killing thousands of people. Gang violence is running rampant in our major cities, mass shooting occurs in churches and synagogues, and international terrorism by radical groups are recruiting individuals to strap on explosives and blow themselves up along with innocent bystanders, including women and children.

The Bible predicts such violence and hatred would ramp up in the last days. How do we cope with all this chaos? To whom shall we look for the answers? The answers are God and His eternal Word. One of the major messages of the Bible is "Do not cast away your confidence, which has great reward." (Hebrews 10:35) In times like this, God wants you to put your trust in eternal things, and not in the instability of temporal things.

You may not agree with what I have said, but if you are a believer in Jesus Christ, I'm certain you will agree that God is sovereign, and His Son Jesus Christ is our High Priest who is making intercession for us. He is able to see us through these difficult and demanding times. It is important that we keep "Looking unto Jesus the author and finisher of our faith." (Hebrews 12:2a)

When you begin *Dancing on the Rubble*, at first it may not be with joy, but with determination to stick with the seven chapters to the end, I am confident that you will be blessed and much better qualified spiritually to face your problems and to fight back if you do. One thing for sure, when your faith is tested, you will be able to withstand the forces that battle against you. Because "greater is He that is in you, than he who is in the world." (1 John 4:4) Don't be afraid to put your problems in God's hand. Fear will eat your faith if you let it, but "God has not given us the spirit of fear, but of love, power and a sound mind." (2 Timothy. 1:7). To become strong in your faith, you must spend time in prayer and Bible study. That is why this path is so important for you. You are going to find your faith increased as you work your way through the text and study guide.

There are seven chapters in the text followed by seven study guide lessons. Each chapter of the text and each lesson of the study guide follow the seven themes represented by seven Biblical characters: Esther (living), Mephibosheth (loving), Abraham (laughing), Solomon (listening) David (learning), Joseph (leaning) and Paul (letting go).

Go with me on this amazing journey into the Word of God and into the lives of Biblical characters and some of the most courageous people you will ever meet.

A journey from:

- anxiety to living
- coldness to loving,
- gloominess to laughing
- deafness to listening
- unwise to learning
- distrust to leaning
- vanity to letting go

Maybe you haven't been on a journey like this one before and you are a little uneasy, but don't be. I know how human nature can cause you to recoil from the pain of others to the point that you say, "I can't go there." Pain is certain for all of us. How we deal with it is optional. Sometimes we cannot do anything other than to lean into it and trust God and His Word.

During our journey we'll explore seven important truths dealing with life itself. The Holy Spirit will lead the way, so just relax and have fun. Just follow Him and He will guide you along the path within the pages of this little book and you won't get lost. To be truthful you will encounter "rubble": debris, ruins, and wreckage along the way. You will encounter even some tragedy, misfortune and heartbreak, but you will also travel to a place of joy unspeakable and full of glory. Don't worry, the Holy Spirit will guide you, and together you will dance on the rubble.

Carl Frederick Buechner, author of *Your Own Journey,* nailed it when he said: "My assumption is that the story of any one of us is in some measure the story of all of us. Everyone has problems, some more severe than others, but how we react to them is really what matters."[3]

Corona Virus (COVID-19) Pandemic: The *Dancing on the Rubble* manuscript was written and sent to the publisher for formatting and proofing and was scheduled for publication at what turned out to be the peak of the pandemic. The timing of its publication allows me to say this about the book: the simplicity, power, relevance, and timing of all the events make it undeniably a work inspired by the Holy Spirit.

Before You Begin

- A study guide follows each chapter that is designed to assist you to go deeper into each of these seven Biblical truths.
- Read the chapter then move to the study guide.
- This *Dancing on the Rubble* study is a Biblical plan that can be used as an individual study and/or small group study. It is my prayer that your outlook on life will genuinely change and your relationship with God will be enriched.
- The Study Guide is divided into seven segments:

    1. Key Quote
    2. Prayer
    3. Inspiration
    4. Backstory
    5. Personal Application
    6. Biblical References
    7. On-line Presentation

- The extended study includes a downloadable video presentation.

How to Get the Most from the Individual Study

This study can be done as an individual one or as a small group study. If you are doing individual study, I encourage you to take advantage of the space that is provided for you all the way through the lesson to record your thoughts, questions, or other insights that the Holy Spirit may inspire you during the weekly session or your own study time between meetings. You will find out later that keeping notes will bless you long after you finish the 7-week study. You will benefit from the Study Guide and on-line video. Together they will provide real helpful information to supplement your studies.

How to Get the Most from a Small Group Study
- Weeks One through Seven: Prior to Meeting
- Skim each chapter and its integrated Study Guide
- Read the chapter as assigned
- Complete the Study Guide questions. Space is provided for your answers and comments, but feel free to use additional pages as needed.
- Resolve to be on time.
- Respect don't Inspect: Respect others' comments and experiences with the Lord.

You are going to have many questions; some you will find answers for and others will take more study and insight. So, don't get discouraged if you don't get your answer immediately. Be patient. Following is an incident from my early ministry that taught me how to ask God questions instead of questioning Him.

Why God?
When our daughter Karen was just beginning to walk, she stumbled on the carpet, fell and hit her head on the corner of the hearth, and cut a gash into her forehead. I grabbed her up into my arms and began praying, asking in a panic: "Why God? Why God? Why, my little girl?" All I heard inside of me was, "Why My Son?" When I heard this inner voice saying, 'Why My Son," my mind was immediately flooded with images of Christ being beaten and crucified. It was then that I was able to connect to how the heavenly Father must have felt to see His Son suffer that unimaginable death on the cross. We hurt, but we forget that our Heavenly Father hurt unbelievably when He witnessed His Son taking the sins of the whole world, past, present and future upon Himself. God turned His face away because He couldn't look upon the sin His Son had to bear. When the Father turned away, Jesus said: "My God, why have you forsaken me?" Why did He say this? He said it so that we wouldn't have to.

Life can be very cruel. The seven principles in this book come at a price because none of them are natural or free. The good news is that we "are more than conquerors through Christ." (Romans 8:37-39) Despite major disappointments in life, i.e., sickness, loss of a job, or the death of a loved one, God has made it possible through prayer and trust in His Word for us to live a victorious and prosperous life.

If Jesus asked why, then it's okay for us to ask why. To ask why is not unspiritual if the "why" is sincere and from the heart.

What you are feeling is important. Ask yourself, "Why do I feel this way? What can I learn from how I feel? Do I "feel" what others are not saying? Don't impose your feeling on others who are also experiencing their own feeling about the lesson.

Remember: Read the chapter of each lesson prior to the next meeting. For the first meeting, read Chapter 1: *Keep Living* before you attend your first group meeting.

*Key Quote: The Key Quote(s) is designed to jumpstart the conversation for the session and build a bridge between both the textbook and the Study Guide themes resulting in a smooth transition between the two. Whether you are a group leader or studying individually, you can begin the lesson knowing that the Key Quote(s) simply contains the central truth of both.

Challenges to Dancing on the Rubble

In every area of life there are challenges one must face and deal with. Below is a short list of some of the challenges followed by a more detailed explanation for each one.

A brief look at some of life's challenges (rubble):
1. Death: (Grief). "And Jesus said to her, "I Am the resurrection and the life. He who believes in me, though he may die, he shall live. And whosoever lives and believes in Me shall never die. Do you believe this?" (John 11:25-26)

2. Divorce: For He Himself has said, "I will never leave you nor forsake you." (5 negatives) (Hebrews 13:5b)

3. Disability: "But He was wounded for our transgressions, He was bruised for our iniquities; the chastisement for our peace was upon Him, and by His stripes we are healed." Isaiah 53:5. "I can do all things through Christ who strengthens me." (Philippians 4:13)

4. Depression: "Why are you cast down, O my soul? And why are you disquieted within me? Hope in God; for I shall yet praise Him, the help of my countenance and my God." (Psalm 42:11)

5. Addiction: "I can do all things through Christ who strengthens me." (Philippians 4:13)

6. Fear: The Bible declares that "God has not given us a spirit of fear, but of power, and of love and of a sound mind." (2 Timothy 1:7)

7. Abuse/Shame: Then He said to the disciples. "It is impossible that no offenses should come, but woe to him through whom they do come! It would be better for him if a millstone were hung around his neck, and he were thrown into the sea, than that he should offend one of these little ones." (Luke 17:1-2)

As it is written: "Behold I lay in Zion a stumbling stone and a rock of offense, and whosoever believes on Him will not be put to shame." (Romans 9:33) The stumbling stone is Jesus and He is the answer to our shame. Our shame was placed upon Him so that we don't have to carry it.

Have you ever had to face one or more of these challenges? If you have, then make some notes below.

Thoughts _____

_____

A More Detailed Look at These Seven Challenges
1. Death/grief:
"Loss is a place where self-knowledge and powerful transformation can happen—if we have the courage to participate fully in the process."[4]

We are not exempt from experiencing many deaths in our lifetime. My mother witnessed the funerals of every sibling on both sides of her and dad's family, including parents and two of her eight children. She experienced these losses before she died two years ago at age 95. Instead of those deaths devastating her emotionally, she was transformed by them.

Grieving is necessary; it is a way to release our emotions and has a healing effect, as long as it is not continued for too long. When Lazarus died, the Bible said, "Jesus wept." (John 11:35; Luke 19:41) It simply means Jesus shed tears. This is considered the shortest verse in the English translation, but not in the original Greek text. The verse is short and maybe its length could be a lesson for some while grieving.

Christians don't grieve as the Bible says others do who have no hope, but we do grieve. I appreciate how the wise man Solomon puts it: "To everything there is a season, a time for every purpose under heaven; a time to be born, and a time to die; a time to kill, and a time to heal; a time to Break down, and a time to build up; a time to plant and a time to pluck what is planted; a time to weep and a time to laugh; a time to mourn, and a time to dance." (Ecclesiastes 3:1-4)

Our society sees death and grief as something of an incursion and disruption in our lives. We Christians believe that death is not an interruption to our lives but a pathway to be with Christ forever. It's all about our depth of faith in God and His Word. The Scripture declares: "Death is swallowed up in victory. O Death where is your sting? O Hades [grave], where is your victory?" (I Corinthians 15:54b-55)

Death and the grief that follows can be a challenge to dancing on the rubble. That challenge is whether we allow death and grief to crush our lives or to transform it. That choice is left up to each of us.

Thoughts _____

_____

2. Divorce

According to Gallup polls and sociologists, one of the greatest scandals of our day is that "evangelical Christians are as likely to embrace life-styles every bit as hedonistic, materialistic, self-centered and sexually immoral as the world in general." The statistics are devastating:

- Church members divorce their spouses as often as their secular neighbors.
- Church members beat their wives as often as their neighbors.
- Church members' giving patterns indicate they are almost as materialistic as non-Christians.
- White evangelicals are the most likely people to object to neighbors of another race. Of the "higher-commitment" evangelicals, a rapidly growing number of young people think cohabitation is acceptable prior to marriage.[6]

Divorce is not an unpardonable sin, but divorce is a major challenge dancing on the rubble because of the many twists and turns it takes emotionally that affects everyone it touches, especially the children. But we can rise above it and get beyond it and someday dance on the rubble! Believe it!

Thoughts _____

_____

3. Disability

Life has its limitations and disappointments, its physical and spiritual challenges. The longer we live the more we understand that fact. I remember the big dreams I had when I was a teenager. Nothing was going to stop me, but something did. It's called aging. I should retract that phrase: it didn't completely stop me. Life, including disabilities and disease, doesn't have to stop us, but it may slow us down.

I am not trying to minimize your pain because that is not my intention. Only you and God know the pain you are going through, both physically and emotionally. I'm saying that God can use pain to work miracles in you and through you in the most unexpected way. Pain and suffering don't guarantee anyone eternal life, but faith in Christ's suffering does.

Stephen Hawking, a famed British physicist, died March 14, 2018. He was seventy-six. Hawking was diagnosed with amyotrophic lateral sclerosis [ALS] at the age of twenty-two and was expected to live only a few more years. He lived virtually his entire adult life with the disease, paralyzed and confined to a wheelchair, but he never gave up probing the mysteries of the universe. However, in all of Hawking's research, he failed to recognize that God made the cosmos. Regarding the brain, he said "I regard the brain as a computer which will stop working when its components fail. There is no heaven or afterlife for broken down computers; that is a fairy story for people afraid of the dark."

Over the years, I have prayed for Mr. Hawking's physical needs and prayed that he would find the Creator of the universe that he loved to explore. His physical computer brain died, but his spiritual computer brain did not. He is more alive now than ever before. If he did not receive Christ before his natural computer died, he has found out that heaven and an afterlife are no fairy story, and I hope he is not afraid of the dark. He is buried in Westminster Abbey in London, England between Charles Darwin and Sir Isaac Newton.

I pray all the time for God to give me strength that I will live up to my potential. I know what pain is. I have some form of physical pain every day, but I have found that I can have peace in the pain. Furthermore, pain can make me look somewhere other than to the outer appearance as Paul put it: "Do you look at things according to the outward appearance." (I Corinthians 10:7) I Samuel 16:7 tells us that God looks at the heart. Because of pain, I look deeper and further than ever before. I pay more compassionate attention to people with disabilities now. I pray for the person walking with a limp, shuffling their feet, sitting in a wheelchair, walking with a walker, or an elderly couple holding hands to maintain balance for one or both. My wife Kaye does this for me now when I walk any distance. I now see below the surface; whereas, before

I saw only above it. Pain has taught me that.

There are two adult members of my family who are featured in the section of this book titled **Some Who Have Learned to Dance on the Rubble**; they are Keegan Kennedy and Novella Brewer. Novella is my sister, and Keagan is my great niece. Novella has lived with the crippling effects of childhood polio, and Keegan was born with cerebral palsey. They are two of the bravest people I know. Keegan's mantra is: "I love my life." When I think of these two, brave people, I am reminded of the words of Winston Churchill who said: "Success is never final; failure is never fatal; it is the courage that counts."

Tim Hansel, author of *You Gotta' Keep Dancin'*, believes that "limitations are not necessarily negative. In fact, I'm beginning to believe that they can give life definition, clarity, and freedom. We are called *to* a freedom of and in limitations—not *from*. Unrestricted water is a swamp—because it lacks restriction, it also lacks depth."[5]

Don't take what I'm about to say as an attack on anyone's faith because I firmly believe that with God all things are possible. (Matthew 19:26) There is nothing wrong with getting on with your life while trusting God for healing or any other miracle. Some people spend their whole lives waiting for something to happen that may never happen. Keegan dances on the rubble when she says, "I love my life!" and takes pencil in hand and colors page after page that takes hours for her to do and then gives them to others with good health but who may have a propensity to "hate their lives" or complain about the least inconvenience. Keegan and others have chosen to dance despite their disabilities. Miracles are possible for those who pray and believe, but isn't it just as great a miracle to trust God no matter what your situation happens to be at this moment?

> "I love my life."
> Keagan Kennedy

Sustaining power is as important as healing power in my opinion. I pray for Joni Eareckson Tada all the time, especially since I was diagnosed with Parkinson's Disease. I find it difficult to turn over in bed at night, but Joni must be turned every four hours by someone else. Read more about them in their book *Joni and Ken, An Untold Love Story* (Zondervan: 2013). My problem is nothing compared to hers. Regardless, those of us who have some type of disability rejoice not so much on achievement but rejoice in the sustaining grace through Christ our Lord who sustains us.

I marvel at Paul's wonderful encouraging letter that he wrote to the Philippians, especially since he was writing from prison. I have visited the prison in Rome where it is believed Paul was held when he wrote the letter to the Philippians who were going through persecution at the time of Paul's letter to them. He writes saying: "And my God shall supply all your need according to His riches in glory by Christ Jesus." (Philippians 4:19) Notice that Paul uses the word need [singular] not needs. I think it is significant because Paul is saying to all of humanity that we have need of a Savior, and when Christ died on the Cross and shed His blood, His death met the need of all past, present, and future human needs all at once.

My Aunt Mae had a pump on her kitchen counter that let her pump water into the kitchen from an underground well. This was considered up-town living when I was a kid because most everyone drew water from a well with a bucket or carried water from a spring nearby. But the pump had a problem; it wouldn't provide water unless she poured water into it first. She had to give it something to get something; the well was unwilling to give its water freely without first being primed. Therefore, the pump was unreliable. Every now and then, one of the family members would forget to fill the pitcher with water to prime the pump. No water to prime the pump meant no water!

Paul said earlier "I can do all things through Christ who strengthens Me." (Philippians 4:13) What Paul is saying to the Philippians is we can trust God to sustain us and meet any need in any circumstance that we face in life. Life also must be primed, too. There is a reservoir of blessings in heaven, but someone is responsible for priming the pump. The way we do that is to "ask, seek, and knock" (James 4:2); "we have not because we ask not" (Matthew 6:32) if we want something from the reservoir of life which is Jesus Christ. All our need is met in God, but we draw from the well of salvation through prayer, fasting, and asking. (II Chronicles 7:14)

Thoughts _____

_____

4. Depression
Today we're hearing a lot of talk about walls. There is a wall that every

person, sooner or later, will face and that wall is depression. For some, the wall will be easier to break through, for others it will not be so easy. Some of the greatest leaders in politics, art, philosophy, medicine, and religion have suffered from depression. The ancients called it "the dark night of the soul."

Eighteen years ago, I endured a depression [a dark night of the soul] which seemed impossible for me to break through. There was a major issue going on between me and the church organization to which I belonged for thirty years. Back then, I would have given anything if I could have avoided it; I had no choice but to face it and trust God for the results. I made it through the trial by the grace of God, and the experience of going through that "dark night of the soul" was worth it.

During the time that I was going through this particular trial, I gave in to having a "pity party" or two. One Sunday morning, a lady came up to me with a mild rebuke; I must have let my feelings show that morning because she said, "Stop complaining; you haven't shed any blood yet." She gave me a lecture about how Christ and the disciples had suffered, and that I was not to expect anything different from what they went through. She probably quoted the following verse to me; "My brethren, count it all joy when you fall into various trials, knowing that the testing of your faith produces patience [endurance or perseverance]. But let patience have its perfect work, that you may be perfect [mature] and complete, lacking nothing." (James 1:1-4)

We all face walls in life. Abraham's depression came from a trial of waiting years for a son. Innocent Joseph's was sitting in jail for at least a dozen years; David's nemesis was King Saul. David hid in the caves of Adullam when fleeing from King Saul. "Now David was greatly distressed, for the people spoke of stoning him, because the soul of all the people was grieved [bitter], every man for his sons and his daughters. But David strengthened himself in the Lord his God." (I Samuel 30:6)

Job's depression resulted from the loss of everything overnight, including his family and all his wealth. He was afflicted with boils and had a wife who encouraged him to curse God and die. He had the world's worst "best" friends who reminded him daily of what a terrible person he was. John the Baptist was beheaded, James was killed with a sword. Peter was crucified upside down, and John the Beloved was exiled on the Island of Patmos. Jesus was betrayed by Judas, denied by his followers, felt forsaken by His Father and was crucified for a world that hated Him. Now these are walls.

The Good News is, Jesus experienced many difficult things, but He overcame them all. He knows the way. He is "the way the truth and the life," (John 14:6) and if we follow Him, we'll make it through every situation we face because He is the door through every wall that leads to eternal life! This is what makes it possible for us to dance on the rubble of depression!

Thoughts _____

_____

5. Addiction

The word addiction can mean many things to many people. Basically, addiction means that a person becomes involved repeatedly with a substance or activity for pleasure or value that is sure to harm them.

A friend of ours, Lawanna Hughes, wrote a booklet entitled, *Freedom, It's a Choice*. She tells about an experience that she had one day. I think it is a perfect analogy of how easy it is to form a habit or addiction and how difficult it is to break it. "One day I was praying with a sweet Christian lady. When we finished our prayers, she told me the following story. 'We used to raise milk fed veal. It's kind of cruel, but we would put a calf in a tiny stall and tie it in, so it couldn't get out of the stall. We fed them nothing but milk. We left them that way for several days, then untied them. By this time, they had become so accustomed to being in the stall that when we untied them, although they could back out of the stall and go free, they didn't. That is the way I was before praying the freedom prayer. I could have backed out of my bondage anytime, but I didn't know I could, so I didn't.'"[7] Overcoming any addiction is never easy.

If you have ever suffered from addiction and gone through withdrawal, or you have watched someone else go through withdrawal, the experience is not a pleasant one. There is no joy in getting clean, but there is a reason for celebration once you do. There is a Christian ministry called Recovery Through Christ founded by Jamie Harper that is a twelve-step program designed to facilitate recovery from a wide variety of troubling behavior patterns. The ministry offers excellent counseling and spiritual guidance for those with alcohol and drug addiction problems.[8]

My father was an alcoholic. There was not much happiness in our lives. We cherished those times when dad was sober which usually didn't last more than a week or two. Ministries such as Celebrate Recovery are wonderful and coupled with prayer it is even more effective.

Our mother was the one in our family who prayed for us. She prayed for dad, and he finally got free for good from alcohol. He committed his life to Christ and was baptized in a little stream near our house. Dad, by the grace of God, finally danced on the rubble, and we rejoiced with him.

> "It is easy to pull a weed; it is harder to pull a tree."
> Lawanna Hughes

I shared our story in my book, *Scars and Stripes, Hope for Adult Children of Alcoholic Families*. It contains amazing stories of miracles of how we survived on God's grace and mother's prayers. Occasionally, there would be moments of humor that brought temporary relief. The key was we never lost hope! Hope is patience with the lamp lit.

Thoughts _____
_____

7. Fear

Fear [a phobia] is real. It is an unpleasant emotion caused by the belief that someone or something is dangerous and likely to cause pain or death, or it can come from a threat causing a person to live in fear, dread, horror, terror, and anxiety.

Babies are born with two fears. The fear of falling [basiphobia] and loud noises [ligyrophobia]. All other fears are learned. To highlight how fear governs our lives, I have listed below a sampling of phobias and their definitions from a list of over one hundred. Hopefully this will help you to see how common fear is and how emotionally harmful it can be.

- Arachnophobia – the fear of spiders (affects women four times more than men)
- Aerophobia – the fear of flying (25 million share a fear of flying)
- Claustrophobia – fear of small/enclosed places (elevators, closets)
- Thanatophobia – fear of death
- Monophobia – fear of being alone

- Tychiphobia – fear of failure (it is the single greatest barrier to success)
- Trypanophobia – fear of needles
- Hippopotomostrosesequippeddaliophobia– the fear of long words
- Theophobia – fear of God

Other fears include the fear of cats, balloons, phobophobia (fear of fear), the number thirteen, buttons, panophobia (fear of everything), bananas, cotton balls, cibophobia (fear of food), catoptrophobia (fear of mirrors), and disposophobia (fear of getting rid of stuff, hoarding), and many, many others.

What, if anything, are you afraid of? Fill in the blanks below.

I am afraid of_____

I am afraid of_____

I am afraid of_____

I believe the main reason why fear is so widespread in our society is because many people have the wrong concept of God. Some see God as ruthless, unreasonable, merciless, impersonal, unnecessary, and un-involved, even totally uncaring about us. Many of these wrong perceptions have their roots in childhood, schools, and our relationships.

Fill in the blanks below.

Why I am afraid of _____

Why I am afraid of _____

Why I am afraid of _____

One of the most vivid memories of my childhood is the time when our family sat in front of the fireplace at night telling "scary" stories. I still remember many of them. In fact, I have told many of them to my children and grandchildren. At the time, I didn't see any harm in passing those stories on to them. What may seem harmless at the time could become a problem later. Phobias can also be caused by a type of child abuse which includes children watching horror movies and playing violent video games. It is almost impossible without divine intervention to reverse [erase] bad experiences and negative impressions from a person's mind, especially children's minds.

The Bible addresses the subject of fear, regardless of the cause, and how to deal with it. The Apostle Paul, writing to Timothy, pastor of the church at Ephesus said, "For God has not given us a spirit of fear, but of power, and of love, and of a sound mind." (2 Timothy 1:7) What is meant by a "sound mind"? The Greek word for it is "*sophronismos* [so-fron-is-mos]. Strongs # 4995: A combination of sos, "safe" and phren, "the mind", and hence, safe-thinking. The word denotes good judgment, disciplined thought patterns, and the ability to understand and make right decisions. It includes the qualities of self-control and self-discipline.

It's possible that young Timothy suffered from fear and timidity; that is why Paul addressed the fear issue. Titus, a contemporary of Timothy and a pastor, had just the opposite temperament, and that is why Paul sent Titus to Crete to pastor a more difficult church, to "set in order the things wanting" [lacking]. (I Timothy 4:14) Paul reminds Timothy that the Holy Spirit's power and the gifts he received by "the laying on of hands" would provide him the enabling power to do the "work of the ministry."

All fear is not bad. For example, the fear of God is Biblical. In this instance, fear means reverence. Godly fear can be a response that warns us to protect ourselves, or not to go to certain places and/or put ourselves in danger. "Fear is a vital response to physical and emotional danger. If we didn't feel it, we couldn't protect ourselves from legitimate threats. But often we fear situations that are far from life-or-death, and thus hang back for no good reason."[9]

Thoughts _____

_____

> Blame and shame are emotions that eat at the soul.

7. Abuse/Shame

I believe shame is one of the most misunderstood emotions that we deal with. Often shame is not something you have done; usually it is something someone has done to you. The Bible says that Jesus "endured the cross, despising the shame . . ." (Hebrews: 12:2) In laymen's terms, Jesus ignored the shame. He paid no attention to it. He waved it off. Jesus carried the sins of the world but would not let Satan load him with blame and shame. There is only a one letter difference between lame and blame, and it's a shame to blame.

Dealing with shame can be a watershed moment in life. It was for Peter when Jesus met with him at the Sea of Galilee. Peter felt ashamed after he denied Jesus in Jerusalem. Peter was so ashamed of himself, especially since he had boasted that he would stay with Jesus even if everyone else deserted Him. Therefore, Peter felt that Jesus would no longer want him to be part of His ministry. So, Peter returned to his fishing trade. It was a watershed moment when Jesus showed up and dealt with Peter's shame. This is an excellent example for dealing with life's circumstances. If you have the courage to confront your shame, you will find Jesus on top of your rubble with an outreached hand to pull you up. If you will take His hand, it will be a watershed moment for you too. Shame is no longer on you; it is laid on Jesus.

The cure for shame is to understand Isaiah 53:6: "All we like sheep have gone astray; we have turned, everyone, to his own way; and the Lord has laid on Him the iniquity of us all." Where is our shame? It is "laid on Him," Jesus Christ. That is what Isaiah said previously in verse five: "He was wounded for our transgressions, He was bruised for our iniquities; the chastisement for our peace was upon Him, and by His stripes we are healed." The provision for our salvation as well as our temporal blessings is received by faith in Christ. He paid it all, and we live in the free grace of Christ with the assurance of eternal life.

For example, Paul, writing to the Philippians from prison, faced the very serious threat of death. Chained to a soldier, he confessed: "For me to live is Christ and to die is gain." (Philippians 1:2) By the way, there is no "is" in this verse in the original text. Paul is saying, "For me to live—Christ, and to die—gain. Notice Paul rose above his circumstances or "rubble" and danced on it with this declaration of faith. That is how it's done! The Bible says, "In all things give thanks for this is the will of

God in Christ Jesus concerning us." (I Thessalonians 5:18) We are not thankful for the circumstance but are thankful that we don't have to live under the circumstance (defeat, fear, depression, and so on) forever.

Here is another interesting way Paul dealt with circumstances and rubble in his life. He writes to the Philippians, "But I want you to know, brethren, that the things which happened to me have actually turned out for the furtherance of the gospel." (Philippians 1:12) The word furtherance is a reference to a strategy used by the military in which a "woodchopper" went ahead of the army and chopped down trees destroying hiding places for the enemy.

Paul did not look on his circumstances from under the rubble, but while he was dancing on top of it. He saw what had happened and was happening to him as a way to defeat the enemy, not only for himself, but for those he could and did help from the circumstance of his prison confinement. In other words, Paul didn't see his captivity and himself chained to a soldier as a problem, but he saw a soldier chained to him. The poor guy had to listen to Paul share the gospel with him and many others day after day for two years. Many were no doubt converted to Christianity. When someone confessed faith in Christ, Paul must have danced on the rubble. That is why he could say, "For I am not ashamed of the gospel of Christ, for it is the power of God to salvation for everyone who believes, for the Jew first and also for the Greek." (Romans 1:16)

When we read about the lives of the early church saints, we realize that they suffered much. Jesus said that in this life we would suffer tribulation, but Jesus also said, "but be of good cheer, I have overcome the world." (John 16:33) The word for tribulation [*thlipsis*] means to crush something like grapes or olives in a press. Jesus doesn't promise us happiness in this life, but He does promise joy. It is joy unspeakable and full of glory because we know that He overcame the world, and by His grace we can too.

Thoughts _____

_____

Q **To access the online supplemental materials for each chapter, go to: *dancingontherubble.com*.**

Chapter 1

Keep Living

Giver of life, creator of all that is lovely,
Teach me to sing the words to your song;
I want to feel the music of living
And not fear the sad songs
Composed of both laughter and tears.
Teach me to dance to the sounds of your world
And your people.
I want to move in rhythm with your plan,
Help me to try to follow your leading
To risk even falling
To rise and keep trying
Because you are leading the dance.
Author unknown

Life begins at conception, living begins at birth. How a life turns out largely depends on the parents who conceived that life and the choices in life we will make as an adult.

The wise man Solomon said:
"To everything there is a season,
A time for every purpose under heaven:
A time to weep
And a time to laugh
A time to mourn
And a time to dance"
Ecclesiastes 3:1, 4

Emotional and physical pain is a given, but how one handles the pain is optional. We must choose joy over pain, and that isn't easy, but it is possible. Viktor E. Frankl, a holocaust survivor, explains in his book *Man's Search for Meaning*, how he turned his suffering around by dealing with it. His terrible suffering in the concentration camp gave birth to what Frankl called logotherapy. He said that a person is motivated by an "inner pull" to find meaning in life. In other words, life has meaning under all circumstances even the most miserable ones.

One of the most revealing statements that Frankl makes which capsulizes his theory is that "when we are no longer able to change a situation, we are challenged to change."[10] To put it another way, human existence is best understood as an in-depth examination of one's own experiences. I was first introduced to Frankl's theory of logotherapy in college. I found the word logotherapy interestng, especially since the Greek word used by the Apostle John for Jesus was *logos* [word]. "In the beginning was the Word [*logos*]. (John 1:1) I'm sure logotherapy works for some people, and it did for Victor Frankl, at least well enough to help him keep his sanity in the midst of the insanity that he endured.

However, my preference is Jesus as the 'logo therapist,' the Therapist with unlimited power. The main difference between Frankl's logotherapy method and Jesus's method is that Frankl's method of therapy provides limited relief for this life, but Jesus, the living Word, goes deeper than just therapy in this life. He forgives sins and brings eternal peace and joy that is eternal life. No other therapy or therapist can do that.

> "There is no box made by God nor us but that the sides cannot be flattened out and the top blown off to make a dance floor upon which to celebrate life." Keith Caraway

Joy is a fruit of the Holy Spirit. He gives us joy in the midst of our pain. When we choose Jesus, we get eternal life by God's free grace. It is free to us, but it cost God His precious Son, Jesus, who willingly gave His life for us. About the subject of grace, Paul writes "for by grace you have been saved through faith, and that not of yourselves; it is the gift of God, not of works, lest anyone should boast." (Ephesians 2:8-9). We're not saved by grace alone, nor faith alone. Salvation is by grace through faith.

When two people dance, one takes the lead. The Holy Spirit must be allowed to lead in the dance if we are going to live a victorious life. When Satan boxes us in, the Holy Spirit can blow off the top and flatten out the sides to make room to dance a victory dance. My mother knew this when she trusted God with the problems that she faced with an alcoholic husband and eight children. She had to have supernatural help from God to do it. Mother realized that the task before her was too big for her to handle, so she cried out to God for help and He heard her. Before she died, at age ninety-five, she witnessed my dad's and her seven living children's salvation. It's a true saying that "God's power is made perfect in weakness." (II Corinthians: 12:9) And that God's grace is sufficient to carry us through any situation or problem. There is always hope! It might encourage you to know that everyone who is a born-again believer has had a past, and all sinners have hope of a future to become a born-again believer. Hope is patience with the lamp lit.

The Trouble with Rubble
A simple definition of rubble is a heap of bits and pieces of anything that once was a thing of beauty but has been shattered either by self or someone else's abuse and left in a heap or cast away [my definition]. Emotional despair, physical challenges, financial stress, and dozens of other life circumstances can deeply challenge our relationships with others and even our relationship with God. But there is always hope for the future to rebuild in Christ Jesus. God can and will restore what Satan has stolen. That is what God promised the prophet Joel: "So I will restore to you the years that the swarming locust has eaten." (Joel 2:25)

We must allow the Holy Spirit to lead the way and not try to lead Him. Whether we find ourselves under the rubble or on top of it, we will find God is already there. That is what the name of God—Jehovah-SHAMMAH means, "Jehovah is there." God wants to help us climb on top of the rubble and restore our joy.

> The focus of this book is not on the rubble, but on how we dance on it.

Life has its many challenges. I have listed only seven challenges to dancing on the rubble. You may identify with one or more of them, or there may be other challenges you will face in the future. No one may know how badly you are hurting right now, but God knows. There is no problem too hard for Him to solve.

My wife, Kaye, and I were horrified as we watched the never-to-be-forgotten events of September 11, 2001. That day is a stark reminder of how quickly disaster can happen. As I was writing today, I realized that today is September 11, 2017. Sixteen years ago today, Kaye and I watched as the two planes flew into the Twin Towers, and we saw them collapse in a heap of rubble. No one felt like dancing then, but things have changed since the day the Towers fell. The terrorists' attack brought our nation to her knees and stirred the patriotic spirit of millions of Americans.

The world watched as President George W. Bush stood on the heap of rubble with fire fighters and other emergency workers, as he shouted into a bullhorn that the perpetrators would be brought to justice and punished for what they had done. The country was determined to rebuild the towers even greater than before. The sacred ground that President Bush was standing on that day was and is and always will be sacred ground to all Americans. It was a sad day when President Bush and rescue workers stood, arm-in-arm, signifying the unity of our country standing on what represented death and great sadness. However, rising above the death and rubble was the deep resolve to rebuild and restore what the enemy had destroyed.

The dream that the Twin Towers would rise again from the rubble became a reality on November 3, 2014, more than thirteen years after the original towers were destroyed. The new towers were completed and reopened for business on that day. The antenna spire on top of the World Trade Center reaches a height totaling 1776 feet, the number corresponding to the year beginning America's nationhood with the signing of the Declaration of Independence on July 4, 1776. Irving Berlin (1888-1989) who wrote "God Bless America" and "White Christmas" and many other popular songs said, "Life is 10 percent what you make it and 90 percent how you take it."

Think about it: living for God is finding the perfect dance partner! Habakkuk is one of my favorite Old Testament prophets. Here's why. He was God's perfect dance partner. His name means embrace. His short Old Testament book contains only three chapters, but they are powerful ones. Living up to his name, he was known for embracing God, others, and the challenging times of his day. When things were tough, he didn't complain about them; he simply believed his God would turn things around. He didn't ignore the bad state of affairs; he just believed that God was bigger than what he faced. He acknowledged the bad and the ugly, chose a positive attitude, and embraced his rubble and danced on it. He "embraced" life. I like that! We can't always choose the music life plays for us, but we can choose the dance partner and how we dance to it. Don't stop dancing! Don't stop living! Get your dance on!

Why Worry?
The reason why we worry is very simple. We have more of a relationship with "what" than we do with "who." Our faith often is in the material, which I'll call the "what," rather than in the "Who:" Jesus the eternal Son of God. A genuine faith is trusting God in the worst of times. This trusting kind of faith is not easy because it deals with the impossible. Living is all about faith—enduring [it doesn't end] faith. I'm not saying that worry hasn't come knocking at my door and that I haven't welcomed it in. But by the grace of God, I have more often refused to worry than I have welcomed it. "Therefore, I say to you, do not worry about your life, what you will eat or what you will drink; nor about your body what you will put on. Is not life more than food and the body more than clothing." (Matthew 6:25) The Greek word for worry is interesting. The word is *merimnao* (mer-im-nah-oh). Strong's #3309: From *merizo*, "to divide into parts."

Philippians 4:9 says, "And my God shall supply all your need according to His riches in glory by Christ Jesus." We are encouraged not to worry about what we need. When we trust Jesus for our need, we will not need to worry about anything. Worry is a sign that we have abandoned our trust in God to supply our need [God's provision]. Once we begin to worry, the need is divided into needs. When that happens, the burden falls on us to take responsibility for worrying about our needs. Once we abandon our faith in God supplying all our "need," worry comes, and the burdens of life become heavy. Peter recognized how life can be almost unbearable when that happens. He said, "Casting all your cares upon Him for He cares for you." (2 Peter 5:7) Ironically, the word *cares* means "to divide the mind." Do you see the comparison? Once you doubt God's promise to supply all your need, your mind is "divided," and you begin to worry about your needs.

We can't do anything to earn our salvation, but we can build our faith in and relationship with our Lord and Savior Jesus Christ by spending time with Him. We can do that simply by setting aside time each day to meet with God. Develop a daily devotional plan to assist you. You may call the plan whatever works best for you and then just do it. The blessings will outweigh any effort you put into it. "If you seek me, you shall find me, if you search for me with all your heart." (Jeremiah 29:12-14)

Rick Warren says, "Life is a gift, but an unopened gift is a worthless gift."[11] Since life is a gift, how do you open it? We open it daily by doing what the Psalmist says: "Enter into His gates with thanksgiving, and into his courts with praise. Be thankful to Him and bless His name." (Psalm 100:4)

You may begin your prayer by saying, "Thank you Lord for life, health and strength, food, clothing and shelter, but most of all for eternal life through your Son, Jesus Christ." Then begin praising God. I enjoy calling out the meanings of God's Hebrew names which I learned from Larry Lea's *Prayer Guide*. To assist you in your personal devotion, acquire a copy of Larry Lea's *Prayer Guide* available via Google.com. Turn to the **Contents** page to find help for "Making a Daily Devotion Plan."

I know it is difficult to believe sometimes the abundance message [prosperity] when the food pantry is empty, hospital bills pile up, and the rent is due, but God's word does not lie. When Satan paints that picture, open the Word of God, believe it, pray it, and confess it and watch God reverse your situation miraculously.

I was browsing through a store recently and a sign caught my eye. It read: "Life isn't about how to survive the storms but how to dance in the rain." That little sign spoke to me and reactivated my faith. I experienced a small miracle when God gave me a great big push in the back to finish *Dancing on the Rubble*. Maybe this quote is speaking to you right now. If it is, pause and let the Holy Spirit lift you out of survival mode and into the dancing mode.

Storms are bound to come into our lives, but when they pass, and they will pass, God will work that storm to your good if you will let Him. And even when natural storms leave devastation behind, how many times have we seen people emerge from the storm, stand on the rubble, and give God praise while proclaiming that they will rebuild and go on living. We can't escape all storms of life whether they are from a personal attack or from a natural disaster. When things come against us, we have four basic choices.

- We can trust God.
- We can rebuild.
- We can resign.
- We can rebel.

When we trust the Lord to get us through the storms, He will get us through every one of them. And when He does you will hear the Holy Spirit say, "Now dance; you deserve it!" Let's rebuild something better than we had before.

Kaye and I have been serving God since we were teenagers, and we have been in the ministry together for over fifty-eight years. Yes, we have had some very difficult times, but we can testify with David, "I have been young and now am old; yet I have not seen the righteous forsaken, nor his descendants begging bread." (Psalm 37:25). Satan may have access to this life, but thank God He doesn't have access to our eternal life. Not even Satan can pluck us out of God's hands. Life has its ups and downs, but even the downside has an upside when we trust our life to the care of Jesus Christ.

Life
Life is like a giant roller coaster
that slowly lifts you up to the sky.
Only to drop you down to the earth
Thinking you are going to die.

Much like a justice balance scale
when life is supposed to be fair.
Justice is nowhere to be found
and is as rare as pure air.
But don't despair dear one
There is an upside to the down.
Consider this, "A tree is best
measured when it is down."* 12

*Quote from a lumberjack and used by the poet Carl Sandburg.

Life is precious so choose life!
   Only that and always!
   At whatever risk.

To let life leak out . . .
   To let it wear away
   By the mere passage of time . . .
To withhold giving it and spending it . . .
   Is to choose nothing! * 13

The oldest living WW II veteran, Richard Arvin Overton, died on December 27, 2018 at 112 years old [eight days short of his 113th birthday]. When he was 110 years old, he was asked what advice he would give others for a long life. His advice was "To keep on living."[14] This answer may seem simplistic, but there is a lot of wisdom in what he said.

There are many people who have stopped living, but who are perfectly healthy. They have no desire to live life to its fullest. Then there are those who aren't physically well who chose to live every day to its fullest. Without the dance, what is the point?

Dancing on the rubble sounds like a contradiction in terms because dancing is normally related to celebration, joy, and victory. Rubble, on the other hand, is just the opposite; it is associated with defeat and sadness and challenges.

> When you dance, dance with a sparkle in your eye!

However, from the Christian viewpoint, dancing can be an act of the will to express confidence in God no matter what the conditions are in life because Christians believe that "all things work together for good" (Romans 8:28b), no matter what. For the Christian, dancing on the rubble is an expression of faith in God that He will turn the situation around. So, Christians can even dance ahead of time like Nehemiah did when he rode his donkey around on the ruin/rubble of Jerusalem at night. Jerusalem had been attacked and its wall and gates reduced to rubble. An aggrieved Nehemiah received permission from King Artaxerxes to go to Jerusalem to restore the city's walls and gates. In the dark hours, he surveyed and assessed the damage. He was certain that the damage would be repaired even before rebuilding began. In his spirit he was dancing on the rubble because of his faith in God.

```
┌────────────────────────────────────────┐
│        Never miss a chance to dance.    │
└────────────────────────────────────────┘
```

Some people have a natural ability to dance. Kaye's father was a coal miner and he danced whenever the opportunity presented itself. His fellow coal miners called him "Boogie" because he would break into a dance no matter where he was, in the mines or out of them. In spite of the dangers he faced daily in the mines, he danced in celebration of life including dancing on the coal mine rubble.

Others Who Danced on the Rubble

Moses and the children of Israel sang a song of triumph over the Egyptians saying ". . . the horse and his rider hath he thrown into the sea." (Exodus 15:1b), "And Miriam [Moses' sister] the prophetess, the sister of Aaron, took a tambourine in her hand; and all the women went out after her with tambourines and with dances." (Exodus 15:20)

King David, elated over the Ark of the Covenant's return to Israel after it was captured by the Phillistines, danced before the Lord in celebration of its homecoming. In Psalm 149, verse 3, David believed others should praise the Lord with dance. "Let them praise Him in the dance; let them sing praises unto him with the timbral and harp." No other King of Israel experienced more heartache or more victories than did David. When he suffered defeat, David got up and danced on the rubble looking forward to the future with victorious eyes.

Elijah, one of the greatest prophets who ever lived and who was carried to heaven in a chariot of fire (2 Kings 2:1-12), was directed by God to go to a certain place and anoint Hazael king of Syria and Nimshi as king over Israel and Elisha as prophet in his place. Where? In the meadow of Abel Meholah which means: "meadow of dancing."

The prodigal son's return as recorded in Luke's Gospel was received with dancing: "Now his elder son was in the field: and as he came and drew nigh to the house, he heard music and dancing." (15:25) I'm sure the father joined in the joyous occasion. Jesus turned water into wine at a wedding in the small town of Cana. (John: 2:1-11) This first record-ed miracle was hailed by a wedding guest as first-class wine. Weddings were a time of joy and celebration with music and dance. Since Jesus was a Jew, he most likely danced at the wedding that day.

Dance, or music, or anything else for that matter, can be done for the wrong reasons. Its reasons can be perverted. It is likely that Hitler danced over the murder of six million Jews as Fuehrer of Germany during World War II. "Dirty Dancing" became a popular form of dance following the 1987 film starring Patrick Swayze and Jennifer Grey. If you do dance, ask yourself the question: "For which reason am I dancing?" Is it for my glory or for God's glory?

Adrian Rogers, a now-deceased pastor of Bellevue Baptist Church, Memphis, Tennessee, once shared a story about how a group of young people tried to encourage a teenage girl to do something wrong. They said to her, "The reason you won't do it is because you are afraid your father will hurt you." She said, "No, I'm afraid to do it because it will hurt my father."[15] Dr. James Montgomery Boice, the late pastor of Tenth Presbyterian Church in Philadelphia, wrote, "Some things are good for us but not pleasant. Other things are pleasant but not good."[16] God's Words are to be obeyed.

A Purpose for Living

So why is there such a difference between those who value life and those who don't? It is as simple as the oldest veteran's answer, the desire "to keep on living." Or as Rick Warren would label it: Purpose! Those who love life believe their life has purpose, and those who do not value life, think they have no purpose. It's as simple as that. If you value life, you will find your purpose. It's like cream that comes to the top of fresh whole milk, but you must separate it into another container for special use.

Where does purpose come from? It comes from God! How do you know what your purpose is? What is it that you always love to do? You can't have purpose one minute and not the next. It is within you. Whether you use your purpose in life, or not, it is left up to you. There is one thing for sure, you have a purpose for being on this planet, and your purpose was given to you by God to live in relationship with Him now and forever. Events come and go in life. Some of them are wonderful events and some are sad and even devastating. But when we're tried by fire, we'll come forth as pure gold as we put our trust in God. Life with a purpose can be measured as we will see in the poem below:

I danced on Friday when the sky turned black.
Oh, it's hard to dance with the devil on your back.
They buried my body and they thought I'd gone,
but I am the dance, and the dance goes on.

Dance, dance, wherever you may be
"I am the Lord of the dance," said he.
"And I will lead you all wherever you may be.
I'll lead you all in the dance said He." [17]

Dancing: An Expression of Life

The Sardis church in the book of Revelation was condemned by Jesus for being spiritually dead. "And to the angel of the church in Sardis write, these things, says He who has the seven Spirits of God and the seven stars: I know your works, that you have a name that you are alive, but you are dead." (Revelation 3:1) The good news is that God has a purpose and plan for each one of us, no matter what life events we go through. Those events don't stop or change God's plan and purpose. There is always an upside to down for us when we trust God no matter what ups and downs we go through in life.

God had a plan for your life even before you took your very first breath at birth. And God's plan and purpose for you is a sealed deal, even after the last breath of air you breathe when you die. There is eternity. Your life doesn't end at death; it lives on in eternity, either in heaven or hell. It's the complete trust in God that, whatever chaos you face in life, He will use it to your good and His glory. It's only a matter of time until this outer body dies. Even Richard Overton, who lived to be 112 years old, experienced death. Despite physical death, there is eternal life beyond this life with Christ in heaven. If we trust in God's love and grace, that trust will make it possible for us to dance on the rubble in spite of our troubles. Sometimes you have to provide your own music. Even the atheist Nietzsche said, "Life without music would be a mistake."

> Sometimes you have to provide your own music.

There are always challenges to our joy, "yet in all these things we are more than conquerors [super conquerors] through Him who loved us." (Romans 8:37)

S.O.S (Save our Souls)

Throughout the Bible there are simple but urgent prayers of "save me," especially in the Psalms. "Save me, O God! For the waters have come up to my neck. I sink in mire, where there is no standing; I have come into deep waters, where the fl ood overfl ows me." (Psalm 69:1-2) S.O.S is recognized as an international distress signal. It is a nautical term especially used by ships to call out for help: "save our ship." It is also associated with such phrases as "save our souls." This last phrase reminds us of the times when we're in distress, and we cry out to our God to "save our souls." We read about the many in the Bible who cried out to their God to save them, especially Peter in the New Testament and Job in the Old Testament.

Job was not exempt from the trials and tribulations that life can bring. And neither are we. God did not allow Job's trial only to watch him fail but to strengthen Job's faith. At the end of Job's trial, he said, "I heard of you with the hearing by the hearing of the ear, but now my eye sees you." (Job 42:5b)

It is also important to see that the affliction of Job, although allowed by God, was a direct work of Satan. (Job 2:2) Peter cried out to Jesus, "save me" when he was sinking in the Sea of Galilee. Jesus reached His hand and saved Peter from drowning. "But when he saw that the wind was boisterous, he was afraid; and beginning to sink, he cried out, saying, 'Lord save me.' And immediately, Jesus stretched out His and caught him." (Matthew 14:30-31a)

An S.O.S distress signal is worthless if there is no one in range who can receive it. The good news is that God is always in range to receive our distress calls. The Bible says, "The righteous cry out, and the Lord hears. And delivers them out of all their troubles. The Lord is near to those who have a broken heart. And saves such as have a contrite spirit. Many are the afflictions of the righteous. But the Lord delivers him out of them all." (Psalm 34:17-18)

The Bible is filled with examples of personal prayers that have a tone of urgency to them. The following are just four examples out of many:

- Exodus 33:18 - Moses said to God "Show me your glory."
- Psalm 139:23 - David said, "Save me."
- Isaiah 6:9 - Isaiah said, "Here am I, send me."
- Judges 16:28 - Samson said, "Strengthen me."

If you serve God faithfully, like Job and Peter did, and millions of others have served, and are serving, God out of a pure love relationship, God will restore your loss like He did Job's. I love Job 42:10, "And the Lord restored Job's losses when he prayed for his friends. Indeed, the Lord gave Job twice as much as he had before." Psalm 34:15 says, "The eyes of the Lord are on the righteous, and his ears are open to their cry!"

The Hedge

Christians are not always aware of how protective God is of His own. Satan certainly realizes it. He must have tried every method within his power to penetrate the "hedge" surrounding Job. Satan admitted to God that Job was hedged in and that he couldn't touch him: "Have you not made a hedge around him, around his household, and around all that he has on every side?" (Job 1:10)

> "We constantly live on holy ground in the presence of the Lord and holy angels." Robert Morgan

The hedge was a complete circle of angels in the form of a shield surrounding Job, his entire family, and all his possessions. It was not a wall as we envision it, such as the wall of China. Job was completely defended by an angelic army in every aspect of his life.

Elisha knew about this hedge of protection. He prayed for God to open the eyes of the young man who panicked when he saw the army of Syrian soldiers surrounding them. "And when the servant of the man of God arose early and went out, there was an army, surrounding the city with horses and chariots. And his servant said to him, 'Alas, my master! What shall we do? So, he answered, do not fear, for those who are with us are more than those who are with them.' And Elisha prayed and said,

'Lord, I pray, open his eyes that he may see.' Then the Lord opened the eyes of the young man, and he saw. And behold, the mountain was full of horses and chariots of fire all around Elisha.'" (2 Kings 6:15-17) The apostle Paul made a similar statement of God's faithfulness. He said, "What then shall we say to these things? If God is for us, who can be against us?" (Romans 8:31)

David knew that angels were a hedge of protection for the servants of God. He said, "The angel of the Lord encamps all around those who fear Him and delivers them." (Psalm 34:7) Believers have life insurance with threefold coverage! Not only are we covered by God's angelic army of angels, we are clothed (filled) with the blessed Holy Spirit and covered with the precious blood of Jesus.

A Good God?

"What good is your God?" This is a question that atheists ask Christians to answer. They say such things as "What good is your God if He allows you and innocent children to go hungry and suffer terrible diseases?" I don't have an answer to that question. But I am certain of two things: first, God walks beside us, and second, He lives in us. This I know for sure. Dr. Fuchsia Pickett, who had a strong 20th century women's ministry, says it like this: "Sometimes God allows things He hates to accomplish things that He loves."[18]

In this book, I have set out to bring you together with events in the Scriptures that literally spiritually illuminates you and increases your faith. Here is an example of one of those life events which illustrates my intent.

"I'm alive!" Maybe you heard about or read about what happened to a little 7-year-old boy named David Rothenberg several years ago. His father went into a fit of anger and went into his son's room and poured kerosene all over the room and the boy and lit him on fire. By a miracle, David lived through the terrible ordeal, although 95% of his body suffered third-degree burns. This left him with virtually no skin. It was estimated at the time it happened that David would undergo 5,000 operations in his lifetime. The doctors estimated that each year they would have to open him up so that he can grow. When I first heard about David's story, I was stunned at his audacity to say: "I am alive! I am alive! I am alive! I didn't want to miss out on living! And that is wonderful enough for me." And so I ask you, what do you and I have to complain about?

> Life is too short to waste
> 'Twill soon be dark!
> Up! mind thine own aim, and
> God speed the mark!"
>> --Ralph Waldo Emerson

Study Guide: Keep Living

Key Quote(s):
". . . I have set before you life and death, blessing and cursing; therefore, choose life, that both you and your descendants may live. That you may love the Lord your God, that you may obey His voice, and that you may cling to Him, for He is your life, and the length of days; that you may dwell in the land which the Lord swore to your Fathers, Abraham, Isaac, and Jacob, to give them." (Deuteronomy 30:19-20)

Begin with Prayer
O Lord, my God, my life, ruler of the universe, bless Your holy name. I seek Your face and Your glory today. I thank you for life, health and strength, food, clothing and shelter, but most of all for the free gift of eternal life through Your only Son, Jesus Christ. I will praise You with my whole heart, mind and soul. I will sing praises to You and lift my voice in witness to Your marvelous grace wherever I go today, anchored in your presence, glory and Holy Spirit that I may value life and keep on living. In the name of Jesus. Amen.

Book: Esther

Author: Unknown

Date: 5th century BC

Inspiration: Read the complete book of Esther.

Excerpts from Esther:
Esther becomes Queen: "So, Esther was taken to King Ahasurerus, into his royal palace. . . . The king loved Esther more than all the other women, and she obtained grace and favor in his sight; . . . so he set the royal crown upon her head and made her queen instead of Vashti." (Esther 21:16-17)

Haman's Plot: "So, Haman said, if it please the King, let a decree be written that they be destroyed. So, the king took his signet ring from his hand and gave it to Haman, the son of Hammedatha the Agagite, the enemy of the Jews. . . the people are given to you, to do with them as seems good to you." (Esther 3:9-11)

Haman's Plot Discovered: "So, the matter became known to Mordecai, who told Queen Esther, and Esther informed the king in Mordecai's name." (Esther 2:22)

Mordechai's Warning to Esther: ". . . do not think in your heart that you will escape the king's palace any more than all the other Jews. For if you remain completely silent at this time, relief and deliverance will arise for the Jews from another place, but you and your father's house will perish. Yet who knows whether you have come to the kingdom for such a time as this?" (Esther 4:13-14)

Esther's Courage: "Then Esther told them to reply to Mordecai: 'God gather all the Jews who are present in Shushan, and fast for me; neither eat nor drink for three days, night or day. My maids and I will fast likewise. And so, I will go to the king, which is against the Jew, and if I perish, I perish!'" (Esther 4:15-16)

Haman Hanged: "Now Harbonah, one of the eunuchs, said to the king. 'Look!' The gallows, fifty cubits high, which Haman makes for Mordecai, who spoke good on the king's behalf, is standing at the house of Haman.' "Then the king said, 'Hang him on it!' So, they hanged Haman on the gallows that he had prepared for Mordecai. Then the king's wrath subsided.'" (Esther 7:9-10)

Truth Triumphs: "The word destroy is the Greek word *louso,* which means that He might undo, outdo, and overdo everything the devil has ever done."

Backstory
The book of Esther is a narrative that takes place over a period of approximately four years which is the account of how God saved His peo-

ple, the Jews, from the powerful king Xerxes who lived in the Persian capital of Shushan. There were Jews still in Persia under Persian rule, even though they were freed fifty years earlier, following seventy years of Babylonian captivity. They had been freed to return to Jerusalem, but they didn't go back.

The story of Esther is about how to "keep living" when the odds are stacked against us. How to confront evil, live to tell about it, and how to celebrate the victory with a dance on the rubble. There are four main characters in this study. They are:

- **Esther** who becomes queen replacing the previously reigning queen, Vashti, who was dethroned. Esther's name means "renewal or light." Her Hebrew name was Hadassah, which means "myrtle."
- **Mordecai** was a near kinsman of Esther who adopted her. He was also a leader to the Jews. His name means "God enlightens." Mordecai was a Jew, and Jews did not bow before any human king. That was why the Babylonian king threw the three Hebrew children into the fiery furnace. They refused to bow to a heathen idol, or to Haman, who was second in command to king Ahasuerus. Mordecai's failure to bow before Haman brought the wrath of Haman upon Mordecai and the Jews. "But Mordecai bowed not, nor did him [Haman] reverence." (Esther 3:2b)
- **Haman** was second in command to the king and wanted to destroy the Jews. His plot was to get rid of Mordecai, Esther, and all the Jews. His plot failed, and he was hung on the seventy-five feet tall gallows that he had prepared for Mordecai. Haman means "tumult." He was an Amalekite, a descendant of Esau.
- **Ahasuerus** was a king whose name means "mighty one." He ruled for twenty years over 127 provinces from India to Ethiopia. He surrounded himself with seven chamberlains who served him, and wise men who knew the Persian law. But they didn't know the "all wise God." (Jude 25). I can't think of anything worse than to be part of a nation or church where God used to be. Esther experienced both God's presence and His absence. The time of Esther was the latter before she confronted evil Haman.

The uniqueness of the book of Esther is that it doesn't mention God. However, Jehovah-*SHAMMAH's* (God is there) imprint is on every page and in every word. There are many analogies one could draw from the book of Esther. No doubt one analogy would be that of the Church, the bride of Christ, that is being prepared to come into the presence of the King of Kings. As the Jewish people were saved from Haman, Jesus also raises up modern-day Esthers and Mordecais to defend His Bride, the Church, from her enemies.

Choosing another queen was not a simple matter. There were established guidelines that had to be followed. It's the same in life. There are instructions in God's Word to help us make the right choices. God said to Israel: "I set before you life and death, blessings and curses, therefore, choose life." Every person, without exception, has chosen or will choose one or the other. The Bible says, "Choose you this day whom you will serve." (Joshua 24:15)

Esther and the other women were required by Persian law to be in preparation for one year before going into the presence of the King. How willing are you to submit to godly authority in a broken, teachable spirit for a lengthy time of preparation before you are sent out on the mission field or ministry of some kind? Esther had learned a way of life by listening to her human authority Mordecai which resulted in life and blessing to the Jewish people. What if she had refused to listen to Mordecai?

Character is what you are in the dark times.

Personal Application: Prayerfully write down your answers to the following questions.

1. What allegory (parable) does the story of Esther represent in the New Testament?

2. How important was it for Mordecai and Esther to work as a team? What if she had not listened to Mordecai?

3. When Mordecai said to Esther: "who knows whether you have come to the kingdom for such a time as this." What did he mean?

4. What did Esther mean when she said, "If I perish, I perish?"

Read Ahead (small group): Read Chapter 2: Keep Loving
The space below is provided to write any thoughts or insights you receive from reading Chapter 2.

_____

_____

_____

Take this Survey
Ranking yourself from 1 to 10, how satisfied are you with the way you are living your life right now? With 1 being "I am very dissatisfied" and 10 being "I am very satisfied." Circle one number.

1   2   3   4   5   6   7   8   9   10

Comments _____
_____

Essential References: John 8:12; I John 5:20; John 14:6; Proverbs 14:27; Proverbs 18:21; Romans 5:10; Romans 6:23; I Timothy 6:12.

Chapter 2

Keep Loving

The night has a thousand eyes,
And the day but one,
Yet the light of the bright world dies,
With the setting of the sun.

The mind has a thousand eyes,
And the heart but one;
Yet the light of a whole life dies,
When love is done.
Francis William Bourdillon

"I have decided to stick with love; hate is too great a burden to bear."
Dr. Martin Luther King, Jr.

Dwight Lyman (D.L.) Moody [1837-1899] was an American evangelist, publisher, and founder of what is known as Moody Bible Institute in Chicago. He was preaching a revival in London, England, and a boy stood up to disturb the meeting. Moody, in his uneducated English said to the young man, "Don't let anyone tell you that God doesn't love you He do." [sic] God loves you because He loves you."[19] God saves us by His grace, and we're kept by His grace. "Now to Him who is able to keep you from falling, and to present you faultless before the presence of His glory with exceeding joy." (Jude 24)

Personal Testimony
Most serious courtships begin with a plan. When I knew that Kaye was the one for me, the one who I wanted to spend the rest of my life with, I began a plan to win her affection. For my plan to succeed, it would take me proving my love for her. I, honestly, didn't know exactly how to do that. I was well acquainted with I Corinthians, Chapter 13, the love

chapter, because this was the text I used in my first attempt at speaking in the church. I had recently discovered God's love for me when I came to Christ, and I was beginning to express my love to Him. I was experiencing a spiritual connection with Kaye somewhat like the love I felt for God. Anyway, it was definitely different from the mere affection that I had felt towards others before her.

I knew I loved Kaye with all my heart, but my plan for us and the future, I admit, was a little short-sighted. My plan barely went beyond the honeymoon stage. It was the same thing when I accepted Christ. I loved God, but I didn't know exactly how to express it. When I look back at my desire to serve God for the rest of my life, my plan was probably about the same as my plan when I got married, short-sighted. I had no concrete plans that extended past the duration of the two-week revival in which I was saved. Despite my naiveté about love, I soon learned that it is all about relationship. It takes time and hard work to bond with your other half. I started to say that you must love the other person as you love yourself, but true *agape* [sacrificial love] love will sacrifice itself for the other person. Kaye and I just celebrated our fifty-eighth wedding anniversary. We have a triangle love affair really; love between the two of us for each other, and both of our love for God. And, may I add, it must be a daily love affair with your spouse and with God.

Love is not about convenience; it is about sacrifice. Sometimes the circumstance makes it inconvenient to express your affection. You really don't feel like sacrificing [dancing]. In fact, you don't know if you love your spouse or God any longer. But time teaches you that God is faithful and that there is "no law against love." God is love, and love wins every time.

> God is love, and love wins every time.

The reason why Kaye and I have been together all these years and can truly say we love each other is because we planned it that way with God's grace and mercy. Our experience has been that love evolves. It certainly hasn't been through our strength and ability alone. We call on God every day to keep us faithful to each other and to Him. Without a quality relationship with God and each other, we couldn't have done it.

God is not mad at you; He's mad about you! If you began every day with: "Heavenly Father, I love You; thank You for loving me," that would be a great start. The way you can tell you love God is because you want to spend time with Him. When I knew I was in love with my wife Kaye, I wanted to be near her. And that desire to be near her has never changed. I can say the same thing about my desire to be near my Lord, Jesus Christ. My 61st spiritual birthday was May 20, 2019.

A sign that love is present in a relationship is when you are fun to live with. I often ask myself this question: "Am I fun to live with?" And I'm not always fun to live with, that's for sure. The stark truth is no one is fun to live with all the time. That is why we must adjust and change when the Holy Spirit reveals the flaws in us and our lives. For example, I used to pray, "Lord, change my children." It didn't work. So, I changed my prayer, "Lord change me." It worked. When I changed, my children changed. Just keep on loving and dancing. Enjoy love; it is the most perfect emotion on earth and in heaven, as long as you don't try to achieve it; instead, you freely give it.

Here is a thought to ponder: the only thing we can be perfect in [by the grace of God] is love. Matthew 5:48 says, "Be ye perfect even as your father is perfect." Matthew is talking about love in the context of this verse. There are only two commandments in the New Testament that we are commanded by Jesus to keep. They are these: love God with all your being and your neighbor as yourself. (Matthew 22:37)

The Apostle Paul defined love in his second letter to the Corinthians (Chapter 13) in which he concluded that of faith, hope, and charity [love], of these three, charity is the greatest. Also, the Bible says, "By this shall all men know that you are my disciples if you love one another." (John 13:35) The Bible declares God is the embodiment of love, that He is Love.

> Love is the only thing that you take with you when you die.

All who have God living inside of them are capable of Godly perfect love. We will never be perfect no matter how many rules we try to keep or how hard we try. However, we have a free will, and we can choose to release the love of God inside of us toward others. Jude says, "Now to Him who is able to keep you from stumbling. And to present you faultless before the presence of His glory with exceeding joy." (v. 24) How is it possible to be presented "faultless before the presence of his glory," when we've all "sinned and come short of His glory?" (Romans 3:23) The answer: God's love! God loves us unconditionally, receptively, and completely. He bought us in sin and brought us out of sin without our help. Read the prophet Hosea's book in the Old Testament, and it will tell you how the love of God makes it possible for a sinner to be presented "faultless before the presence of His glory with exceeding joy."

I made a statement to our son Howie recently when we were talking on the phone. I said, "Love will take you to the edge." I don't know what that statement fully means, but my first thought was God's love will take you as far as you are willing to go to know and obey Him more fully. I believe the edge is found when we are willing to forgive ourselves and others. Forgiveness is not easy; if it were, everyone would do it. "Forgiveness is me giving up my right to hurt you for hurting me." (Anonymous) Love will sacrifice its reputation to love and reach the lost. It will risk life and limb to love others.

Recently, a twenty-six-year-old missionary named John Allen Chau was killed by an isolated tribe on the North Sentinel Island near India. His effort to preach the gospel of Jesus to the people there has been criticized by many in the media. He has been accused of breaking the law and acting foolishly. Chau believed that eternal life is in Jesus Christ and that is why he went there and risked his life to reach the people. I realize that there are pro's and con's as to whether he should have done so. We may judge him harshly, but I don't think God will.

> Love will sacrifice its reputation to reach the lost.

The physicians and nurses who risk their lives to go to Africa where the Ebola outbreak has killed over 5,000 people to date, do so out of *phileo* love [brotherly love]. The Bible says, "Greater love [*agape*] has no one than this, than to lay down one's life for his friends. (John 15:13) The greater love is God and Jesus who is perfect, pure *agape* love [sacrificial] laid down His life for His friends (us). He demonstrates the greater love when He died for us. When we become perfect in Christ [forgiveness] through the spiritual birth, then we too can love perfectly. God's love makes the difference. The difference is the difference! We dance on the rubble to express not to impress.

"There can be no greater calling than to truly care for others, even to the laying down our lives for them. Nothing will edify the Church more than the gifts of the Spirit operating through love and in line with the teachings of God's Word."[21] Religion condemns, puts up walls, divides, puts works before grace, and points its members toward earth [their own interests] not heaven [God's free gift]. Religion says, "You must pay." God says, "I paid [*tetelestai*] in full." Love releases; religion binds and imprisons.

God's love is expressive in a special way when Scripture says that we have been adopted into the family of God. Beth Moore, well-known author, Bible teacher, and founder of Living Proof Ministries tells of a conversation she had with her husband Keith when their adopted son was four years old. The adopted son said that he didn't have a father, and Keith said he didn't have a son, so Keith made a proposition to the four-year-old. "If you will be my son; I will be your father." "It's a deal," said the little boy. That is the way we become a part of God's family. ". . . I really do love love. What I don't love is people who don't feel loved to feel like losers."[23] God offers to be a father to us and we agree to be His sons and daughters. That covenant or that mutual agreement between us and our God makes it possible for us to rejoice regardless of life's circumstances. The Holy Spirit can give us the power and will to dance on the rubble in spite of the circumstances.

A New Commandment

The first time love is mentioned in the Bible is in Genesis 22:2. "Then He said [to Abraham], 'Take now your son, your only son Isaac, whom you love, and go to the land of Moriah, and offer him there as a burnt offering on one of the mountains of which I shall tell you.' "The reason why this event in Scripture is so powerful is because it is a presage to God sacrificing His Son on Calvary. That is the same place where Abraham was told to offer up his son Isaac. Spring forward 4,000 years from Abraham to Jesus who, on the night of the Last Supper and His betrayal, said in His final instructions to His disciples, "A new commandment I give to you, that you love one another: as I have loved you, that you also love one another. By this all will know that you are My disciples, if you have love one for another." (John 13:34-35) The goal of every Christian is to love God and others, but it is easier said than done. Sometimes we can only love some people at a distance. Again, the stark truth is, at times, we aren't too loveable ourselves.

The following conversation between Jesus and Peter is one of the most revealing stories in the Bible regarding the love relationship between God and man. It is about how Jesus skillfully loved Peter back to "fishing for men" instead of fishing for fish. The setting is the Sea of Tiberias in Galilee. Peter is joined with Thomas called the Twin, Nathanael of Cana in Galilee, the two sons of Zebedee, and two other disciples. Remember, this was after Peter denied Jesus three times. Jesus had called Peter to follow Him from this same geographic location, the Sea of Galilee. "Simon Peter said to them [the other disciples], 'I am going [back to] fishing.' " (John 21:1-2) It is important to define two important Greek words for "go" at this point. They are the words: *hupago* and *ago*.

1. Peter uses the Greek word *hupago* [to go and not return] instead of the word *ago* [to go and return]. The use of the word *hupago* means "I'm going and won't be coming back."
2. The word *ago* means just the opposite. It means "I'm going but I plan to return." Peter's plan was to go back to fishing. He didn't see any future in following Jesus.

The word that Peter used for boat is *ploion* which meant that the boat was a large boat. Apparently, Peter did not do away with his fishing business when he first followed Jesus. He didn't burn that bridge behind him when he answered Jesus' call. Peter was an influential leader among his people. So, when he said he was going fishing, "they said to him, we are going with you also, and they immediately went out and got into the boat." (John 21:3) Our decisions always influence others whether for good or bad.

Peter and his fellow fishermen were coming into shore after a night of fishing without catching any. Jesus stood on the elevated shore overlooking the men in their boats. He asked them if they had caught any fish and they said, "No." Jesus said, "Cast your nets on the right side of the boat and you will catch some." (John 21:5,6) It was not unusual for someone to stand on the shore and spot schools of fish and direct boats to them. They obeyed Jesus, and they caught a net full totaling 153 fish. John the beloved said, "It's the Lord."[v. 7] Then, Peter took off his outer garment and plunged into the sea. He got ashore before the others. There was a fire with fish and bread cooking. Jesus invites the disciples to eat. This was the third time Jesus had appeared to His disciples after His resurrection.

The mission Jesus was on, which was to bring Peter back into the fold, was about to begin. Peter was a "key log" in a "log jam" that was hindering God's plan. Something had to be done to get Peter unstuck so that he could get back to fishing for men. As we noted earlier, when Peter said he was going fishing, the others followed him. So, after they ate breakfast, Jesus began to challenge Peter's love for Him. He said, "Simon, son of Jonah, do you love [agape] Me more than these [the fish]?" Peter answered, "Yes Lord, you know that I love [phileo] you. Jesus said, "Feed My lambs." (John 21:15-17)

Jesus said the same thing the second time using the word agape and Peter uses the same word phileo the second time. This time Jesus changes from lambs to "tend my sheep." Jesus asked Peter twice using agape for love. Peter answered with phileo. The third time Jesus asked Peter if he loved Him, Jesus used Peter's own word for love [phileo], questioning if Peter had even a fondness for Jesus. This grieved Peter because Jesus asked him the third time if he even loved Him with a phileo love. Again, Jesus told Peter to shepherd His sheep. (John21:17)

Peter eventually received the revelation of what agape love was because Peter used the agape/agapao words nine times in his writings. And according to ancient writings, Peter was crucified upside down, at his request, considering himself unworthy to be crucified upright as Christ was on the Cross. Now, that is sacrificial love! One can't say "No" and "Lord" in the same breath.

> There is nothing like love because God is love, and there is no one like Him.

The Love Chapter: I Corinthians: 13 in Action

The author of the following passage quoted from *The South African Pioneer* is anonymous and does an excellent job of putting the love message into the modern vernacular.

"If I have the language perfectly and speak like a native, and have not His love for them, I am nothing. If I have diplomas and degrees and know all the up-to-date methods, and have not His touch of understanding love, I am nothing. If I am able to argue successfully against the religions of the people and make fools of them, and have not His wooing note, I am nothing. If I have all faith and great ideas and magnificent plans, and not His love that sweats and bleeds and weeps and prays and pleads, I am nothing. If I give my clothes and money to them, and have not His love for them, I am nothing.

If I surrender all prospects, leave home and friends, make the sacrifices of a missionary career, and turn sour and selfish amid the daily annoyances and slights of a missionary life, and have not the love that yields its rights, its leisures, its pet plans, I am nothing. Virtue has ceased to go out of me. If I can heal all manner of sickness and disease, but wound hearts and hurt feelings for want of His love that is kind, I am nothing. If I can write articles and publish books that win applause but fail to transcribe the Word of the Cross into the language of love, I am nothing."

Loving and Sharing

There isn't much that I can do, but I can share my bread with you, and sometimes share a sorrow, too—as on our way we go.

There isn't much that I can do, but I can sit an hour with you, and I can share a joke with you, and sometimes share reverses, too—as on our way we go.

There isn't much that I can do, but I can share my songs with you, and I can share my mirth with you, and sometimes come and laugh with you—as on our way we go.

There isn't much that I can do, but I can share my hopes with you, and I can share my fears with you, and sometimes share a prayer with you—as on our way we go.

There isn't much that I can do, but I can share my friends with you, and I can share my life with you, and oftentimes share a prayer with you—as on our way we go." (Anonymous)

Love and Hugs

In the middle of an ordinary day, God demonstrated His love to me through a little girl named Patsy. I had gone to Little Caesars to pick up a pizza. When I entered the place, there was a man and a young girl standing at the register placing their order. If you've ever been to Little Caesars, you know that most of the food is prepared ahead of time and placed in a warmer so that when an order is sold another one is immediately baked to replace that one. For whatever reason, the order that the man placed had to be baked on the spot. The father moved to my right and sat down, leaving only the little girl, who I would guess was nine or ten years old, at the counter with me. When her father sat, the child wrapped her arms around my waist and laid her head on me and said, "I love you." I was really surprised by both her words and actions.

"What is your name?" she asked. I told her my name and asked her what her name was, and she replied, "Patsy." Then, I realized she had Down Syndrome. After our exchange, her father said, "Come Patsy, sit with me." She took her arms from around me and joined him. As I passed them when leaving, I said to her father, "She sure is a sweetie." And he replied, "She sure is." I closed the door behind me, and I heard an inner voice say, "That was Me who just hugged you." I knew that voice was God speaking to me.

When I shared this story with others, I was told that it is the nature of Down Syndrome children to hug and love on people. If that is true, and I'm not disputing it, I still believe God hugged me through Patsy. Whether Patsy's show of affection was natural or learned, it doesn't matter to me. I'm convinced that God hugged me that day. The amazing thing to me is that God knew I needed a hug, and who He chose to demonstrate that love through was Patsy, a beautiful little girl. God You are amazing! Thank You!

Deeper in God's Love

Let's go a little deeper into the subject of just "keep loving." I believe that before love can be given it must be received. That is why we should hug our kids from the moment they are born until the day they die, or we die. Why was Patsy so love-giving? I believe she must have been shown lots of affection by others. I sensed that Patsy's father adored her.

Do you know that love and the power of the Holy Spirit are one? The Greek word [*epipipto*] that is used for the infilling of the Holy Spirit is also used for the love embrace of the father toward his prodigal son. "But when he was yet a great way off, his father saw him, and had compassion, and ran, and *fell* on his neck, and kissed him. (Luke 15:20) [italics mine]. I adore the comparison of these two events because it speaks of our Heavenly Father's first loving us, and then He fills us with the love with which He first loved us. He hugs us, then He hugs us again. Hallelujah! I like to think that the extra hug from God is so that we would have an extra dose of love to share with others.

This same identical Greek verb is used by Luke in Acts 10:44: "While Peter yet spoke these words, the Holy Ghost *fell* on all them which heard the Word [italics mine]. Imagine God's arms hugging the world as He demonstrates His Love for humankind. Imagine, too, God hugging you in the same way as the father who hugged his prodigal son. When we are saved, we personally receive God's first hug. We receive another from Him, when we are filled with the Holy Spirit. How quickly we forget God's love for us. How soon we forget to love others, or just forget to tell people we love them. And how soon our love becomes cold as did the Ephesus church. "Nevertheless, I have this against you, that you have left your first love." (Revelation 2:4a).

If you give someone a big hug today, don't be surprised if you receive a hug from someone yourself. Don't be shocked if that hug comes from a child as precious as Patsy.

Love is an action word that is easier to share than define. Why? Because whenever we define love, automatically we draw a boundary or line around it. Therefore, defining love is a problem because God is love, and He is omnipresent, infinite, and unlimited. Who can define God? Yes, God is love, but try defining either, or both. It's impossible! That is why when you show love to the best of your ability, there is no law against or a limit to love. So just keep loving.

In his book *Learning to Love*, David Alsobrook, put together a forward-looking exercise for improving and deepening your understanding of love.[21]

Instructions:

1. First, <u>verbally</u> place your name in each blank.
2. Next, <u>verbally</u> place "Jesus" in each blank.
3. Last, <u>verbally</u> place "Jesus in me" in each blank.

Do not rush or say the words only in your head. Take your time and be sensitive to the impressions of the Holy Spirit. Go through the exercise slowly and aloud.

_____suffers.
_____is patient.
_____is kind.
_____is not jealous.
_____does not brag.
_____is not arrogant.
_____does not act unbecomingly.
_____does not seek his own.
_____is not provoked.
_____keeps no records of wrongs He receives.
_____does not rejoice in unrighteousness.
_____rejoices with the truth.
_____bears all things.
_____believes all things.
_____hopes all things.
_____endures all things.
_____never fails.
_____does not harm.
_____covers a multitude of sins.

Write your thoughts about how helpful this can be in your spiritual development.

_____

_____

_____

Jesus witnessed to the woman at the well in Samaria, and she went into town and told the people about Jesus. The people came running out to see, and when Jesus saw them coming, he said to his disciples: "lift up your eyes;" in other words, "look at all the souls coming out from Samaria."(John 4:35) What would you see if Jesus opened your spiritual eyes right now?

Why is God's love for others so important in our lives? The love of God constrains us to share His love with others; that's why! For every Christian there are 8.5 non-believers in the world.[26] The underlying reason for living is to pass on the love of God to them. The Sardis church in Revelation was condemned by Jesus for its lack of life. "And to the angel of the church in Sardis write, these things, says He who has the seven Spirits of God and seven stars: I know your works, that you have a name that you are alive, but you are dead." (Revelation 3:1) If there is no love, there is no life.

The difference between a corpse and a person is life. A spiritually dead church is a detriment to the kingdom of God. There's nothing that concerns me more than being part of a church where God used to be. I heard a story of a little boy whose cat had died, and his father tried to console his son telling him that his dead cat was now in heaven with God. The boy replied, "What does God want with a dead cat?" What use does God have for a dead, loveless church? None.

Dr. W.A. Criswell, who was the pastor of the First Baptist Church, Dallas, Texas, confessed Christ at the age of ten, committed to the ministry at the age of twelve, and was licensed at the age of seventeen. He was on vacation in North Carolina with his wife, Anna, and they decided to visit a church on Sunday morning. Dr. Criswell said the service was spiritually dead. The people were not friendly, and the sermon was boring. He said that the only time the people showed any signs of life was when the service was dismissed, and they gathered up their purses and coats. Following the service, the Criswells went to a restaurant to eat. There the people were friendly; the music was lively, and there was a lot of excitement. Dr. Criswell said there was no altar invitation given at the previous church service, or at the restaurant but, he said, if the restaurant had given one, he would have joined it.[22]

I read a book recently entitled, *The Insanity of God by* Nik Ripkin, who happens to be from my home state of Kentucky. Nik, along with his wife Ruth, worked faithfully in the mission field for over thirty years. After the death of their young son, the couple spent several of those years interviewing over seven hundred persecuted Christians, asking them the question "IS JESUS WORTH IT"?[23] The book was made into a movie. The story is about two ordinary people who learned how to love, obey, and trust Jesus when it didn't make sense at all to do so.

Could a simple definition of love be doing something for someone at some inconvenience to ourselves? The Ripkins found that the seven hundred persecuted believers testified that following Jesus, regardless of the persecution, was worth it! Many of these believers were from China.[22] China has witnessed tens of millions who have recently come to Christ. Some have accepted Christ through dreams.

Your own ministry and labor of love may not make sense right now, but it will some day when you hear the Lord Jesus say to you, ". . . well done good and faithful servant: you have been faithful over a few things. I will make you ruler over many things. Enter into the joys of your Lord." (Matthew 25:23) Are you feeling the love? Share that love with someone today.

Study Guide: Keep Loving

Key Quote(s):

"For God so loved the world that he gave His only begotten Son, that whoever believes in Him, should not perish but have everlasting life." (John 3:16)

"Love like you've never been hurt." Jentezen Franklin

Loved: *Agapao* (ag-ah-pah-oh). Strong's #35. God's unconditional love. Love by choice and by an act of the will. Love transends everything! Love will go with you into heaven without changing.

Begin with Prayer

O Lord, my God, lover of my soul. I praise You with my whole heart for Your love for me. I put my trust in You today. Help me, dear Lord, to return that love in some way to You and those whom I meet today. Preserve me, O God and my family from the evil one. Enlighten my eyes to see what You see. Put a sparkle in my eyes and a smile on my face that others may see You in me. Infuse me with Your love for others the Good News of eternal life. Give ears to my prayer and help me to keep on loving. In the name of Jesus. Amen.

Book: 2 Samuel

Author: Unknown

Date: Around the division of Israel into two kingdoms in 931 BC

Inspiration: 2 Samuel 9:1-12

[1] Now David said, "Is there still anyone who is left of the house of Saul, that I may show him kindness for Jonathan's sake?"

[2] And there was a servant of the house of Saul whose name was Ziba. So, when they had called him to David, the king said to him, "Are you Ziba?" He said, "At your service!"

[3] Then the king said, "Is there not still someone of the house of Saul to whom I may show kindness of God?" and Ziba said to the king, "There

is still a son of Jonathan who is lame in his feet."

⁴ So, the king said, "Where is he?" And Ziba said to the king, "Indeed he is in the house of Machir the son of Ammiel, in Lo Debar."

⁵ Then King David sent and brought him out of the house of Machir the son of Ammiel, from Lo Debar.

⁶ Now when Mephibosheth the son of Jonathan, the son of Saul, had come to David, he fell on his face and prostrated himself. Then David said, "Mephibosheth?" And he answered, "Here is your servant."

⁷ So David said to him, "Do not fear, for I will surely show you kindness for Jonathan your father's sake and will restore to you all the land of Saul your grandfather; and you shall eat bread at my table continually."

⁸ Then he bowed himself, and said, "What is your servant, that you should look upon such a dead dog as I?"

⁹ And the king called to Ziba, Saul's servant, and said to him, "I have given to your master's son all that belonged to Saul and to all his house."

¹⁰ "You therefore, and your sons and your servants, shall work the land for him, and you shall bring in the harvest that your master's son may have food to eat. But Mephibosheth your master's son shall eat bread at my table always." Now Ziba had fifteen sons and twenty servants.

¹¹ Then Ziba said to the king, "According to all that my lord has commanded his servant, so will your servant do." "As for Mephibosheth," said the king, "he shall eat at my table like one of the king's sons."

¹² Mephibosheth had a young son whose name was Micha. And all who dwelt in the house of Ziba were servants of Mephibosheth."

Backstory
David's kindness to Mephibosheth

The story of Mephibosheth's birth began around 1015 BC; Father: Jonathan; Children: Mephibosheth, grandson of King Saul, and Micha.

Second Samuel deals with David coming to the throne of Israel and the forty years of his reign as king over Judah. The kingdom was split into two kingdoms, Israel and ten tribes to the north, leaving the southern kingdom with only two tribes Judah and Benjamin. Our study begins with the death of Saul and Jonathan at the battle of Mount Gilboa. Gilboa is a mountain range in northern Israel overlooking the valley of Jezreel. This is the place King Saul, the first king of Israel [Mephibosheth's grandfather], led a charge against the Phillistines. Three of Saul's sons were killed, and he fell on his sword. When David heard the news of their deaths, he cursed Mount Gilboa.

You may remember learning that the house of Saul and the house of David didn't get along, and over time the house of David became stronger and the house of Saul became weaker. After seven and one-half years, the nation was unified under David. In this story of Mephibosheth, the son of Jonathan, was injured at the age of five. His injury happened when he and his nurse were fleeing for their lives after the death of Jonathan and King Saul at the battle of Jezreel. Apparently, the nurse dropped Mephibosheth and he became lame in both feet.

Life has its surprises. Sometimes the surprise is pleasant and sometimes it isn't. But for Mephibosheth, his life took a one hundred eighty degrees positive turn in one day. This study is about Mephibosheth's good fortune. His "dark night" turned into a bright sunny day all because of the friendship and love between David and Jonathan, that was passed down through them to Jonathan's son, Mephibosheth.

The first sign of friendship and covenant between Jonathan and David happened when David was brought to King Saul after David killed the Phillistine giant. (1 Samuel 17:57-58) The Bible says, "Now when he had finished speaking to Saul, the soul [life] of David was knit to the soul [life] of Jonathan and loved him as his own soul [life]. Saul took him [David] that day and would not let him go home to his father's house anymore. Then Jonathan and David made a covenant, because he loved him as his own soul [life]." (1 Samuel 18:1-3)

David and Jonathan renewed their covenant privately in a nearby field to guard against being seen or overheard by Saul, who hated David. Their covenant is recorded in 1 Samuel 20: 11-23. The private covenant Jonathan entered into with David, on behalf of his descendants, was an irrevocable vow. (1 Samuel 20:16, 17) It assured Jonathan that when David came to the throne, he would not only spare his descendants but also his wealth. This covenant between David and Jonathan was indisputable. It is amazing in both its intent and in its action. It stands unequaled anywhere in history with regard to human kindness and friendship.

We pick up the story when David becomes king, and he inquires if there is anyone in the house of Saul that he can show kindness to.

Covenants and Friendships

It is human nature to make friends from the most casual ones to the most intimate ones. Friendships are important because we all need someone with whom to share both our problems and successes. A recent Harvard study concluded that having solid friendships in our lives even promotes brain health. Friends help us deal with stress and help us make better lifestyle decisions that keep us strong. Friendship also allows us to rebound more quickly from health issues and diseases. It is equally important to our mental health.[24]

Spiritually, God values covenants. He made a covenant with Noah following the flood with the rainbow as a sign that He would not destroy the world with another flood. This is the unconditional first of five covenants between God and man. (Genesis 9:8-17) The covenant God made with Abraham (Genesis 12:1-3) birthed Israel as a chosen people and promised Abraham that he would have a son in whom all peoples would be blessed. That promise included the Son of God, Jesus Christ, who sealed the final covenant with His own blood on the cross for the salvation of all mankind.

Personal Application: Prayerfully write down your answers to the following questions.

1. In your own words, what are some of David's feeling when he heard about Jonathan's death?

2. What was David feeling when he showed kindness to Mephibosheth the grandson of Saul?

3. What do you think was David's reason for bringing Mephibosheth to eat at his table?

4. What are some of the thoughts and feelings you had when Mephibosheth referred to himself as "a dead dog" [a person of no value]?

Read Ahead (small group): Read Chapter 3: Keep Laughing

The space below is provided to write any thoughts or insights you receive from reading Chapter 3.

_____

_____

_____

Take this Survey
Ranking yourself from 1 to 10, how satisfied are you with your love for God and love for others?

1 being: "I seldom show love to others." and 10 being: "I show love to others a lot." Circle one number.

1   2   3   4   5   6   7   8   9   10

Comments _____

_____

Essential References: I Corinthians 13; I John 4:8; I Peter 4:8; John 15:13; Romans 5:8; I Corinthians 6:14; I John 4:7-8; Zephaniah 3:17; Luke 6:35; Ephesians 5:25; Nehemiah 9:17; Psalm 107:8-9.

Chapter 3

Keep Laughing

I love to laugh, and I enjoy hearing others laugh. Maybe it is because I didn't laugh much when I was a child. I was raised with the parental warning, "If you laugh today; tomorrow you will cry." When I visited my cousins or my friends and we laughed, I wondered if tomorrow I would get a whipping or something worse. Honestly, some of the happiest memories that I have now are the times when I was free to laugh. Laughter is a God given emotion that relieves stress. It decreases stress hormones and increases immune cells which fight off diseases. Laughter releases endorphins that are nature's way of making us feel good. The Bible says that "A merry heart does good, like medicine. But a broken spirit dries the bones." (Proverbs 17:27-28)

Let's Laugh!
Someone said to me recently, "Imagine a handful of dirt next to a small rib. Can you tell me what that represents? I said, "No." He said, "It's Adam and Eve's baby picture." Now that is funny.

The story goes that Satan challenged God to a creation duel. God agreed to the challenge, but he said to Satan, "You ought to go first because I have already created Adam." And for this reason, Satan scooped up a handful of dirt to do his miracle, but God stopped him and said, "No, no, no, Satan, you have to use your own dirt."

Sow Joy, It's a Choice
Don't be afraid to laugh and express your joy when you can. The expression on the face of one who receives a gift, or when children are surprised with a toy, is priceless. Right now, can you think of more than one occasion when someone brought joy to you, or when you brought joy to someone else? These memorable moments last forever. What is your favorite happy memory?

He Danced for Joy

One of our fondest memories happened to Kaye and me years ago. It happened during the Christmas holiday. We lived in Chicago which was several hundred miles from where both of our parents lived in southeastern Kentucky. Our second child, Karen, was born on Thanksgiving and we didn't know if the doctor would allow us to travel home for Christmas. Usually a new mom was not allowed to travel long distances for the first six weeks. We desperately wanted to be home for the holiday. We called home and explained to our family that we didn't know if the doctor would release Kaye to travel in time for us to come home. Tears were shed, and we waited for the doctor's verdict. To our surprise, the doctor released Kaye just in time for us to make it home for Christmas. We were thrilled, and decided to surprise our parents, so we didn't call them.

When we arrived, Kaye's father was coming down the front steps of the house. He saw us, and he ran back up the steps and into the house yelling, "Kathryn (Kaye's mom) I told you they would come! I told you they would come! I told you they couldn't stay away from home on Christmas!" When he came back out of the house, he began to dance on the front porch. He was known to love to dance. He was a coal miner and his coworkers called him "Boogie" because he would break out dancing at the slightest opportunity. His joyful little dance that Christmas was a gift that still lives in our memory today. Johnny (Kaye's dad) learned how to dance on the rubble. Try it. Dance. It works!

Don't Be So Serious

Recently, I decided to spray some wasps that had invaded the barn. I thought that I would not have a problem according to the instructions on the spray can because the spray could reach up to thirty feet. I positioned myself in the doorway where I could spray the huge wasp nest located on the other side of the building. One by one, I wiped them out.

Then I sensed that there might be wasps on the side of the building where I was standing. I slowly lifted my head and right above my head was a huge nest covered with dozens of black wasps. I decided to spray them and then run for my life. I sprayed the wasps, but I forgot about my Parkinson's. Wasps began falling all around me. If my escape had been captured on film, it could have been featured on *America's Funniest Home Videos*. As part of a Parkinson's patient's therapy, the doctors tells us to "move fast and speak loudly." I did both. We have to laugh at ourselves sometimes. I tell people that the upside to my Parkinson's is I get free milk shakes. I hope that statement doesn't offend anyone, but there is a bright side to everything if you'll just take time to look for it. Any disease is serious, but we must not allow it to take away our joy.

> "Laughter has no accent." Paul Lowrey

Dr. Larry Crabb, a well-known psychologist, seminar speaker, Bible teacher, author and founder/director of New Way Ministries said, "We can count on God to patiently remove all the obstacles to our enjoyment of Him. He is committed to our joy. Satan will do whatever he can to destroy your joy."[25]

I enjoy hearing laugher, especially that of my children, grandchildren, and, yes, great-grands. If I get pleasure out of hearing them laugh, don't you know our heavenly Father enjoys hearing a sweet laughter coming from us, His children? We have proof in Deuteronomy 28:47 that followers of God usually have difficulty serving Him with "joy and gladness of heart." And that doesn't sit well with God.

Senator, John McCain died on August 25, 2018. It was a sad day for all of us. However, almost every news outlet mentioned how he loved to laugh. There are photos of him laughing and videos of him telling funny stories. The one I remember best is the answer he gave to a talk show host when he was asked if he had trouble sleeping after he lost his bid for president to Barcak Obama. His answer was, "No, not at all, I slept like a baby. I slept for two hours, woke up and cried, slept for two hours, woke up and cried." And when he told the joke he laughed louder than anyone else. The former Vice President, Joe Biden, said in an interview, "John was known for his wit and humor." George H.W. Bush died

November 30, 2018, and his funeral was held on December 5, 2018, in Saint Martin's Episcopal church in Washington, D.C. The main speaker, Reverend Dr. Russel Levenson, Jr., also shared how much the former president enjoyed humor.

Outbursts of Laughter

We often experience laughter in the most surprising places and at the most unexpected times. Today Kaye and I took a trip to a small town about thirty miles from us to do some shopping. We decided to have a sandwich first, so we stopped at a fast food restaurant when we arrived. There were only Kaye and I and two senior ladies in our area of the restaurant. The early crowd had left, so some tables were still being cleared except for a table near the two ladies. It so happened that our booths were back-to-back so that we were able to hear every word the ladies said, including their outburst of laughter. The more they laughed, the more we laughed. They were not annoying. In fact, Kaye and I joined in, but they didn't realize it. They were so caught up in their own heart-to-heart conversation it could have been thundering and it would not have mattered to them.

As Kaye and I got up to leave, we turned around and said to the ladies, "You all are having too much fun." Of course, they laughed. But here is the rest of the story. We introduced ourselves, and one of the ladies named Cora said that her husband died one year ago. Betty, the other lady, said her husband had died only two months ago. Cora, who had had more time dealing with her loss, said that she was there to cheer up her friend Betty.

I shared with the ladies the main reason why their laughter caught our attention. I said I am writing a book entitled *Dancing on the Rubble* and one of the chapters is called "Keep Laughing." That is when Betty said something that made our day. She said, "My candle (meaning the death of her husband) may have gone out, but the sun is still shining!" Now that's dancing on the rubble!

A Happy Heart

Joy and gladness are marks of Christianity. "Because you did not serve the Lord your God with joy and gladness of heart for the

> "The surest mark of a Christian is not faith, or even love, but joy"
> Samuel M. Shoemaker

abundance of everything. . . ." (Deuteronomy 28:47)

When you read Chapter 28 in Deuteronomy, it will sober you to "examine yourself to see if you are guilty of overlooking God's bountiful blessings." Verse 47 is the one I mentioned above. It is a serious matter when anyone snubs the abundance of God's blessings. Take the time to look up Chapter 28 and read what happened to Israel for not serving the Lord with joy and gladness of heart.

It is estimated that 350 million people internationally suffer from depression. It is also estimated that 20% of college students think of committing suicide.[27] One suggested remedy for depression is reading novels. Reading is supposed to get the mind off what is depressing and involved in the novel's plot and characters; thus, changing one's thoughts that will, in turn, supposedly heal the emotions. This sounds logical and probably helps some people. However, if depression is a spiritual matter, the best remedy is to have a relationship with Jesus Christ. Christians can become depressed as well as non-Christians. However, "a spirit of fear" breeds worry; worry breeds depression. Depression is rooted in the spirit of fear. Ultimately, depression must be dealt with at the root of the problem, fear. Only God can remove that.

I believe the reason why many Christians are so gloomy and depressed all the time is because they are not secure in their salvation. They are spiritually blinded to God's "great grace" (Acts 4:33; John 1:16) which span's the universe many times over. Grace is one of the most misunderstood doctrines of the Bible. Most Christians believe that initially salvation begins with grace, and that is true, but grace doesn't stop there. From the moment we become a born-again Christian, grace powered by the Holy Spirit, explodes outwardly in our lives to do extraordinary feats. Grace is more than an acrostic [G(od's) R(iches) A(t) C(hrist's) E(xpense)].[26] Grace is that too and so much more; the "more" is what I'm referring to. Paul calls it "grace for grace." Extraordinary things happen following our acceptance of Christ. The money that was ours before, now belongs to God. Now we want to give it away to missions or to feed the hungry. Now we have a desire to attend church and to lift-up the downtrodden when before we disliked doing these things.

We can be saved and not enjoy the assurance that we are Christians because we feel we are not good enough. So, we resort to trying to earn our salvation by doing good deeds to earn favor with God. Only then we can feel we are worthy of heaven. That is no way to live. We need to stop doing and start trusting in what Jesus has already done for us. If Jesus did it all, what more can we do? Instead of working for our salvation, we must learn to trust and try laughing for a change. It does us good like a medicine!

Think About This

There are 365 "fear nots" in the Bible, one for each day of the year.

In Philippians 4:12-13, Paul makes the following declaration, "I can do all things through Christ who strengthens me." Paul means that no matter what he faced in life, whether he had plenty or was in need, Jesus was his source. His source was in Christ not in the power of the mind to just think it. I believe in positive thinking, but not in the mind's ability to create whatever it can conjure up. "As a man thinks, so is he" (Proverbs 23:7; Romans 1:18-23) doesn't mean that he can have or be anything he can think of. I believe God can do all things, but I certainly can't do all things. I can do all things through Christ who strengthens me, but I can't do anything without God. I do believe God can do miracles for me, in me, and through me if I trust Him fully. And He can also do the same for you!

I am by no means saying God's power is limited. He is Omnipotent! But no matter how I believe I can be an astronaut and go to the moon, it's not going to happen. The problem with just positive thinking alone is that it focuses on the power of the mind, and what it can do rather than the mind being subject to God and what He can do through the mind. We can do all things, but nothing without him. Now that is positive thinking.

People with Disabilities Laugh, Too

I hope the following anecdote will lift your spirit today. People with disabilities laugh, too. Herb, who is the host of our Monday night home Bible study, shared an experience he had last week. You would love Herb. He is a kind, gentle man. He and I share a mutual neurological disability, namely, Parkinson's Disease. Maybe that is why his story interests me and makes me laugh.

Our prayer/Bible study group averages a dozen attendees. The meeting is casual and relaxed which gives the members the opportunity to share their personal testimonies. One night, Herb shared a personal event that had recently happened to him. He said that he had driven himself to the gym where he exercises and takes voice therapy. He still drives and is especially proud of his Subaru pickup truck. He had parked in a reserved spot, locked the truck doors, and went inside for about an hour then returned to his vehicle. He was shocked to find that someone had stuck a large flag decal on the rear window of his truck. Herb was peeved to say the least. Mumbling under his breath, he decided to remove the decal immediately and not wait until he got home to do it. So, he reached inside of his front trouser pocket and took out his trusty Buck pocket-knife and scraped the decal off the window.

Herb removed it, which took some time, then he pushed the "unlock" button on his key fob to open the door. But the door wouldn't unlock. Now, he thought, "the vandals who put the decal on my truck window must have put glue in the lock." So, he rushed to the door to open it manually. Herb inserted the key into the lock and tried to turn it. No luck. Frustrated, he began to push the fob repeatedly. He thought maybe the fob was broken, or its battery was dead. To his delight, this time it worked! Just not on the truck that he had scraped the flag decal off. It worked on another Subaru truck in the next aisle over. Herb had scraped the decal off someone else's truck window and was trying to open the wrong truck door. Embarrassed, he glanced around then left the scene in a hurry, sort of. I'm sure the owner of the other Subaru is still scratching his head and wondering how in the world his flag decal disappeared from his truck's window.

Some of my favorite humor comes from actual statements made on insurance forms by people who had been in a car accident. Following are just a few of them.

- Coming home, I drove into the wrong house and collided with a tree I didn't have.
- The guy was all over the road: I had to swerve a number of times before I finally hit him.
- I pulled away from the side of the road, glanced at my

mother-in-law, and headed over the embankment.
- In my attempt to kill a fly, I drove into a telephone pole.
- I had been driving my car forty years when I fell asleep at the wheel and had an accident.
- The pedestrian had no idea which direction to go, so I ran over him.
- The telephone pole was approaching fast. I was attempting to swerve out of its path when it struck my front end.

> Laugh like no one is watching. Because they're not, they're checking their cell phone.

Twin brothers went to the Air Force recruiter to enlist in the service. The recruiter said to one twin, "What kind of skills do you have? Any military skills?" "I'm a pilot," the twin replied. The recruiter was thrilled to hear that the first twin was a pilot. He stood up and shook the young man's hand and said, "Welcome to the Air Force." The officer turned to the other twin and said, "What about you?" He said, "I chop wood." "I'm sorry, we don't need wood choppers," replied the recruiter. "But you enlisted my brother," the twin replied. "Yes, but he is a pilot." The twin shook his head and said, "I know that, but I have to chop the wood before he can pile it!"

A nephew went to South America on vacation, and he sent his uncle a beautiful bird. It was at Christmas time, so the uncle thought the nephew had sent it to him for Christmas dinner. When the nephew returned, he asked his uncle if he had received the bird that he sent him. The uncle replied, "Yes, and it was delicious." "Oh, no, you didn't eat the bird I sent to you; it cost me a fortune and, besides, it could speak two languages." "Then why didn't the bird say something?" the uncle asked.

Laughter is a bit like a "rest" in music. It allows us to pause. It is as important as the notes on the scale, but it is not meant to be the focus of the piece of music. Enjoy a good laugh. It relieves stress, lightens the heart, and tunes the soul. "If you laugh, you will cry later." This philosophy is a joy killer. Those who teach this do more harm to children than they may realize. The practice may be an innocent one by which parents keep their children quiet, but it can have a harmful psychological effect on their emotions. If children are to grow up happy and emotionally healthy, they must grow up with an appreciation for wholesome laughter.

A good thing to remember and a better thing to do, is to work with the construction gang, not with the wrecking crew.

Just One More

A man received a telephone call from his wife just about the time she was to fly home. Their conversation went something like this:

Wife: "How's my cat?"
Husband: "Dead. He fell off the roof."
Wife: "Oh, honey don't be so honest. Why didn't you break the news to me slowly. You've ruined my trip."
Husband: "What do you mean?"
Wife: "You could have told me my cat was on the roof, and when I got to Paris, you could have told me he was acting sluggish. Then when I called from London, you could have said that he was sick. And when I called from New York, you could have said that he was at the vet. And when I arrive home you could have said he was dead."

The husband had not been exposed to such protocol, but he was willing to learn.

Husband: "O.K.," he said, "I'll do better next time."
Wife: "By the way, how is my mom?"
Husband: (silence) Then he said: "Uh, she's on the roof."

Joy to the World

Let's talk about joy. What is it and where does it come from? First, let us look at what joy is not. It is not humor or laughter. A person may have a good sense of humor and be very outgoing, laugh a lot and not have joy. On the other hand, a person may be suffering for various reasons and still have joy. So, how does a person get joy? I am convinced that joy comes from total confidence [trust] in God and God's Word on the wings of the Holy Spirit. I wrote a book of poems entitled: *Sow Joy, It's a Choice*. Serving God ought to be joyful.

Listen again to this stern warning that I quoted earlier: "Because you did not serve the Lord your God with **joy and gladness of heart**, for the abundance of everything. Therefore, you shall serve your enemies. . . ." (Deuteronomy 28:47-48a) It is a Biblical fact; joy can keep the adversary away. To the contrary, a lack of joy can be an invitation for a visit from him. I agree with Samuel M. Shoemaker, a former Episcopal priest who was also affiliated with Alcoholics Anonymous, that joy is the defining mark of a Christian. He said: "The surest mark of a Christian is not faith, or even love, but joy."

Godly Joy in Action

Polycarp, one of the great early church fathers (69-155 AD), was burned at the stake for his Christian testimony; not a happy occasion, but he had joy. Joy comes from within. He died a martyr's death, refusing to be nailed to the stake. He said, "He who grants me to endure the fire will enable me also to remain on the pyre unmoved, without the security you desire from the nails." Tradition has it that the Roman soldiers stabbed him when the fire failed to touch him.

Joy, Paul says, is a fruit of the Spirit. (Galatians 5:22, 23) Nehemiah said, ". . . so don't sorrow, for 'the joy of the Lord is your strength.'" (8:10b) Habakkuk said, "Yet I will rejoice in the Lord, I will joy in the God of my salvation." (3:19). Polycarp got his joy from knowing he was secure in Christ and that joy is what gave him the strength to glorify God even while being burned at the stake.

God's Joy

Could there be another side to joy that we haven't heard much about? I believe there is. We emphasize the joy that we have, and it's true we do have joy, but does God have joy and where does He get it from? I believe our heavenly Father's joy comes from knowing we are His children. His joy is us! And our joy (strength) comes from knowing that we are a joy to Him. Hallelujah!

Look at this Scripture again with the emphasis on Lord. 'The joy of the Lord (His joy) is our strength." Our strength is the joy of knowing how much our heavenly Father loves us and rejoices over us. Just like we rejoice over our own children. "The Lord God in your midst. The Mighty One, will save; He will rejoice over you with gladness, He will quiet you with His love. He will rejoice over you with singing." (Zephaniah 3:17) "But be glad and rejoice forever in what I create; For behold, I create Jerusalem as a rejoicing, and her people a joy. I will rejoice in Jerusalem, and Joy in My people; the voice of weeping will no longer be heard in her." (Isaiah 65:18-19). Other references: Luke 17:15; Hebrews 12:2.

Dance with Joy

Strong's definition for joy is even more revealing. Habakkuk 3:18, joy, *gil (geel)*: Strong's #1523: "To joy, rejoice, be glad. *Gil* contains the suggestion of "dancing for joy" or "leaping for joy," since the verb originally meant "to spin around with intense motion." Strong's definition should lay to rest the idea that joy is just a quiet inner peace. There are many Biblical examples showing that joy can be emotionally and outwardly expressed.

David danced before the Lord when the Ark of God was brought from the house of Obed-Edom to Jerusalem: "Then David danced before the Lord with all his might." (II Samuel 6:14a). David's joyful dancing was frowned upon by Michal, his wife, who was also Saul's daughter. "And as the Ark of the Lord came into the city of David, Michal . . . looked through a window, and saw King David leaping and dancing before the Lord: and she despised him in her heart." (II Samuel 6:16)

I know what you are thinking. How can a person dance with joy when the circumstances are severe? There are times when circumstances can be devastating. The dancing is delayed until God's Word soaks into the spirit and mind. Then miraculously the strength comes, and we get up, put the problem under our feet, and go joyfully on our way. What happens is, given a little time, what we thought was a bad thing becomes a blessing. I have experienced this truth many times over. Bad doesn't always have to turn out bad if we trust God to "work it (the bad) together for good." (Romans 8:28.)

Lewis B. Smedes, in his book entitled *How Can It Be All Right When Everything Is All Wrong,* said: "You and I were created for joy, and if we miss it, we miss the reason for our existence. If our joy is honest joy, it must somehow be congruous with human tragedy. This is the test of joy's integrity: is it compatible with pain? Pain has a loud voice!"[27]

> Only the heart that hurts has a right to joy.
> Lewis B. Smedes

As I wrote the last sentence, my mind went back to when I was a child and how mother punished us children for some mischief we'd done. She would take us by the hand, so that we couldn't escape. Then she would swat us with some branch that she broke off from a shrub. She would swing, and we would run around and around in a circle screaming bloody murder. It was comical to watch but it wasn't any fun to experience. So, in the process, we didn't enjoy the pain nor the dance either. But it was amazing how it improved our hearing and behavior.

The reality of joy doesn't require physical or even verbal expression because those with a disability may not be able to express it, but joy may be seen in the sparkle of the eyes and the peaceful glow on the face which speaks volumes of inner joy. My paternal grandmother Dora had a stroke and could not move a muscle. I remember sitting by her bedside fanning her because we didn't have air conditioning. I was only a child, but I can still remember the love that I felt emanating from her toward me. Even though she couldn't speak to me, the Holy Spirit spoke for her to me through her eyes. Love is contagious, and eyes can speak lovingly, or they can speak loudly without making a sound.

Some types of secular dance appear to be akin to Biblical dancing, but they are not the same. For example, one can dance to celebrate an event but have nothing to do with a God given anointed dance that comes from the Holy Spirit. The former one can be just to have a good time, make a statement, or enjoy oneself, or just for exercise. I'm not saying dancing to celebrate some event is wrong; I'm saying that there is generally a difference between dancing to the glory of God and dancing to celebrate a life event. There's a big difference between the two.

"Wacky" Dance

A good example of dancing solely for personal satisfaction appeared on ABC's Evening News broadcast on October 3, 2013. Reporter Jon Donavan, aired a YouTube video of Marina Shiffrin, an Internet sensation doing a "wacky dance" entitled "I Quit." She recorded it at 4:30 a.m. in her employer's office. The video went viral, racking up over six million hits at the time of the October airing. The place where Marina worked was a company that marketed ways to get messages out to the public. She got her job resignation message out all right, not only to her boss, but also to the Internet world. Although Marina's dance was labeled as "wacky," she got her message across and appeared to be enjoying herself immensely.

Meadow of Dancing

The following Biblical example is one hundred and eighty degrees opposite of "wacky" dancing. The meaning of the birthplace of Elisha is, Abel-Meholah, which means "meadow of dancing." The meadow of dancing is found in the story of Elijah anointing Elisha in I Kings 19:11-21. Elijah is discouraged. He has been battling with Ahab and running from Jezebel who seeks to take his life. He has gone through three-and-one-half years of drought; he hid in a cave; he wanted to die; an angel fed him. Then God gave him a new assignment. ". . . the Lord said to him, 'Go return on thy way to the wilderness of Damascus and when thou comest, anoint Hazael to be king over Syria: And Jehu the son of Nimshi shalt thou anoint to be king over Israel: and Elisha the son of Shaphat of Abel-Meholah shalt thou anoint to be prophet in thy room [place].'"

The "meadow of dancing" is a soft place to land and a place for anointing and restoring joy. When you are born again, you are born in the "meadow of dancing." Then you can climb above the rubble and dance on it and continue dancing into the future.

Speak Joy Through Tears

Godly men and women shed many tears over their lifetime. William Paul Young, author of The Shack, said this about tears: "Never discount the wonder of your tears; they can be healing water and streams of joy. Sometimes they can be the best words the heart can speak." Tears are a wonderful gift from God, but only we can make them. Sad tears are not meant to be forever. See poem entitled *Tears* in the "Poems For and From the Soul" section.

Tears are precious no matter whether they are tears that wash away hurt or are tears of joy that express what we cannot express with words. Be cautious with tears; don't get stuck in tears of lamentation only. God desires to answer our prayers, and He can't answer them if we get stuck in "why" or "how long" all the time. Even sad tears are a gift of God. There are even tears of remorse. The shortest verse in the Bible, "Jesus wept" (John 11:35) was over the news that His good friend Lazarus had died. Everyone has shed those tears, but they are not forever. Some people make their joys ordinary events and their troubles great occasions. Satan wants us to get stuck in defeat and despair forever. "If we confess our sin, He is faithful and just to forgive us our sins and to cleanse us from all unrighteousness." (1 John 1:9). God is our righteousness. That is why He is called *Jehovah-tsidkenu*, Jehovah our righteousness. And because of His gift of righteousness, we rejoice!

King David Got It Right
Notice the spiritual progression of King David's prayer in Psalm 13. He goes from weeping to singing in six short verses. He says, "How long, O Lord will you forget me forever: How long will You hide your face from me? How long shall I take counsel in my soul? Having sorrow in my heart daily? How long will my enemy be exalted over me? (vv.1-2). Then, David shifts gears from lamenting to asking. He asks God to "consider and hear me, O Lord my God; enlighten my eyes [put the sparkle back]. Lest I sleep the sleep of death; lest my enemy say I have prevailed against him, lest those who trouble me rejoice when I am moved." (vv.3-4) Observe how David shifts from lamenting, to asking, then to praising God. He advances to dancing on the rubble. Listen to the joy in his words, "But I have trusted in your mercy; my heart shall rejoice in your salvation. I will sing to the Lord, Because He has dealt bountifully with me. (vv.5-6)

Outlook Is Critical
To get beyond brokenness and sadness we must do our part. One thing we can do is speak the Word of God over ourselves and over our circumstance. God told the prophet Joel to speak strength over Israel. ". . .let the weak say, I am strong." (Joel 3:10) King David "made [encouraged]

himself strong in the Lord." (I Samuel 30:6) Another thing we shouldn't do is spend more time looking backward instead of looking forward. Sometimes we have to look backward to go forward. But a rearview mirror was not invented to spend more time looking into it more than looking into the windshield. If you do, you'll certainly wreck. Laughter, joy, and praise are garments that never go out of style. Joy and praise are always forward-looking. Praise can be for past victories; however, two-thirds of our praise is about the present and future. God gave us joy and laughter to relieve stress and to make life enjoyable, but Christians don't laugh enough; laughter is often a minor exercise in our daily lives.

Pray, Praise, and Dance

In the April/May 2015 issue of *Neurology Now*, a publication of the American Academy of Neurology is an article entitled "Calm Your Mind." It lists five smart ways to stress less. In short, they are the following:

1. Look inward (meditate, pray)
2. Get moving (exercise, dance)
3. Binge (on anything that makes you laugh or feel good)
4. Listen to or play music (releases calming hormones)
5. Develop friendships (boosts cognitive abilities)

Following these tips can help us reduce the stress in our lives, leaving us with more energy to find the joy and the laughter inside. Laughter and joy are as necessary to human beings as is the air we breathe and the food we eat. Keep laughing, find moments of joy in life each day, pray to see and find the positive and good in your life that will help you to dance, and keep dancing on the rubble.

I close this chapter with one of my favorite humorous stories (as told by David Stone on January 29, 2013 at *youtube.com*.)

Billy Graham was returning to Charlotte after a speaking engagement, and when his plane arrived there was a limousine there to transport him home. As he prepared to get into the limo, he stopped and spoke to the driver.

"You know," he said. "I am 87 years old and I have never driven a limousine; would you mind if I drove it for a while?"

The driver said, "No problem. Have at it."

Billy gets into the driver's seat, and they head off down the highway. A short distance away sat a rookie state trooper operating his first speed trap. The long black limo went past him doing 70 in a 55-mph zone.

The trooper pulled out behind the speeding limo and easily caught up to it. The limo driver pulled over, and the trooper then got out of his patrol car to begin the ticketing procedure. The young trooper walked up to the driver's door, and when the glass was rolled down, he was surprised to see who was driving.

He immediately excused himself and went back to his car and called his supervisor. "I know we are supposed to enforce the law. . . but I also know what I should do because I have stopped a very important person."

The supervisor asked, "Is it the governor?"

The trooper said, "No, he is more important than that."

The supervisor said, "Oh, so it's the president."

The trooper said, "No, he's even more important that."

After a moment, the supervisor finally asked, "Well then, who is it?"

The trooper said, "I think it's Jesus, because he's got Billy Graham for chauffeur!"

Remember: a merry heart does good, like a medicine.

Study Guide: Keep Laughing

Key Quote: "A merry heart does good, like a medicine, but a broken spirit dries the bones." (Proverbs 17:22)

Begin with Prayer
O Lord, the lifter up of my head, the joy of my life, hear the meditation of my heart today. I praise You for the joy of my salvation. I serve You with joy and gladness of heart for the abundance of everything. I greatly rejoice in Your strength. You have given me my heart's desires. I asked for eternal life and You freely gave it to me. I asked for the gift of the Holy Spirit and You baptized me with holy fire. I asked You for healing and you healed my body, soul, and spirit. Your abundant blessings are too numerous to name. They are as the stars of heaven. You have not withheld any good thing from me. I exceedingly rejoice in Your faithfulness, mercy, and grace. To You, O Lord, my God and Savior I lift my praise. Thank You for putting joy and holy laughter back into my life and thanks to You I can keep on laughing and dancing on the rubble. In Jesus' name I pray. Amen.

Book: Genesis

Author: Probably Moses

Date: 1440 BC

Inspiration: Genesis 17:15-17

[15] Then God said to Abraham, as for Sarai your wife, you shall not call her name Sarai, but Sarah shall be her name.
[16] And I will bless her and also give you a son by her; then I will bless her, and she shall be a mother of nations.
[17] Then Abraham fell on his face and laughed, and said in his heart, shall a child be born to a man who is one hundred years old? And shall Sarah, who is ninety years old, bear a child?
[In spite of their new names being changed from Abram to Abraham and Sarai to Sarah, it would be thirteen years before God affirmed His

Covenant with Abraham. Abraham would be 100 years old and Sarah would be 90 years old, when their promised son, Isaac, would be born.]

Genesis 18:1-15
[1] Then the Lord appeared to him by the terebinth trees of Mamre, as he was sitting in the tent door in the heat of the day.
[2] So he lifted his eyes and looked and behold, three men were standing by him; and when he saw them, he ran from the tent door to meet them and bowed himself to the ground,
[3] and said, "My Lord, if I have now found favor in Your sight, do not pass on by Your servant.
[4] Please let a little water be brought and wash your feet and rest yourselves under the tree.
[5] And I will bring a morsel of bread, that you may refresh your hearts. After that you may pass by inasmuch as you have come to your servant." They said, "Do as you have said."
[6] So Abraham hurried into the tent to Sarah and said, 'Quickly, make ready three measures of fine meal, knead it and make cakes.'
[7] And Abraham ran to the herd, took a tender and good calf, gave it to a young man, and he hastened to prepare it.
[8] So he took butter and milk and the calf which he had prepared and set it before them; and he stood by them under the tree as they ate.
[9] Then they said to him, "Where is Sarah your wife?" So, he said, "Here, in the tent."
[10] And he said, "I will certainly return to you according to the time of life, and behold, Sarah your wife shall have a son." [Sarah was listening in the tent door which was behind him.]
[11] Now Abraham and Sarah were old, well advanced in age; and Sarah had passed the age of childbearing.
[12] Therefore Sarah laughed within herself saying, "Shall I have pleasure, my Lord being old also?"
[13] And the Lord said to Abraham, "Why did Sarah laugh saying, 'Shall I surely bear a child, since I am old?'
[14] "Is anything too hard for the Lord? At the appointed time I will return to you, according to the time of life, and Sarah shall have a son."
[15] But Sarah denied it saying, "I did not laugh," for she was afraid, and He said, "No, but you did laugh!"

Backstory

This study is about Abraham and Sarah who were visited by three angels sent from God with an incredible message. They were to have a son when Abraham was almost one hundred and Sarah ninety years old. All laughter is not funny! That is at first, anyway.

Consider this: according to nature, it wasn't physically possible for Abraham and Sarah to become parents at their ages. There had not been any pitter-patter of little feet in their tent in years, at least not since the birth of Ishmael fourteen years previously. Abraham had fathered a son, Ishmael, by Hagar, the handmaid of Sarah [at Sarah's request]. However, when Isaac, the son of promise (Genesis 18) was born, Sarah became angry and insisted that Hagar and her son Ishmael both be cast out. (Genesis 21:8-21)

It's worth noting that it was not until the feast of Isaac's weaning that Sarah insisted Abraham send Hagar and Ishmael away into the wilderness (Genesis 21:9-10). He did so the next day. We don't know exactly how old Ishmael was when he was sent away with his mother Hagar, since there is no exact age known when Isaac was weaned. Ishmael's age could have been between seventeen and nineteen years.

Imagine yourself seeing three men at the door. The Hebrews did not distinguish a difference between angels and God because they are His messengers in human form. They have knocked on the door in the middle of the day. You are not aware that they are messengers from God. You invite them in, and they have some good news for you. The angels inform you that your wife will conceive and bear a son to you in your old age. Abraham and Sarah didn't faint at the news, but they did laugh. Probably out of both astonishment and disbelief. What do you think?

Here is the same scenario in today's vernacular.

Abraham is cooling off at the door of his tent. He is now one hundred years old; his hearing has diminished so much that Sarah had to loudly repeat things. He is awakened from a nap by Sarah's half excited and half hysterical tone of voice. Abraham doesn't understand what she is so excited about. Sarah arrives with some odd-looking apparatus in her hand, holding it closer than usual to him due to his failing eyesight.

"What is it Sarah, what is that you are holding in your hand?" Abraham asked. "It's a pregnancy test," Sarah said out of both astonishment and disbelief. "What!" Abraham said. "Who's pregnant?" "Me, you silly old man. I am!" replied Sarah. "You remember the visitors we had last year; they told us we would have a child." Sarah had to repeat her statement about the angel's visit because his hearing and his memory had faded over the past couple of years. "We're going to have a son," she said. Abraham laughed a belly laugh, and this time it was out of joy in God's faithfulness. Sarah joined him. Such harmonious laughter had not been heard in their tent for at least a year, at the announcement that Abraham and Sarah were told they were going to have a child by Sarah, not Hagar. Then it was a laughter of astonishment and disbelief. Today was different. "By the way, what will we call our son?" Abraham asked. "Isaac! Don't you remember the angel told us his name would be called Isaac because we laughed when the angel told us we would have a child at our age?" "Isaac," Abraham said, "The name Isaac means laughter." Now that is funny!"

It takes sixty-four facial muscles to make a frown, but only thirteen to make a smile. Phillips Brooks, American Episcopal clergyman and author of the lyrics to "O' Little Town of Bethlehem," said: "A religion that makes a man look sick certainly won't cure the world!" A merry heart does good, like medicine, but a broken spirit dries the bones." (Proverbs 17:22) Laughter heals as a medicine heals. Medicine comes in different shapes, colors, strengths, and for different reasons, and so does laughter. It comes in all sorts of emotions. This startled me. I associated laughter only with comedians or funny jokes and stories.

We laugh when we are sad, happy, angry, disappointed, astonished, hysterical, and even in disbelief. We can laugh out of anger because we didn't get the expected raise or promotion we thought we should have. We can laugh at our 100th birthday party, knowing that we have lived way beyond life expectancy. It seems that we can laugh out of every possible human emotion. But it is important to note what the above Scripture says a **merry heart** does good, like a medicine. This indicates to me that "dancing on the rubble" comes out of the joy of the Holy Spirit. It is certainly not the same laughter as in the movie "Dumb and Dumber."

We may laugh hysterically when someone totally continues to disregard our feelings. To understand our emotions, we need to understand ourselves. Why do we get angry when someone cuts us off in traffic? I've had this weird thought: what if we could hear all the conversation at once of disgruntled drivers in one of our major cities? God does!

It's therapeutic to laugh. Laughter may be the safety valve that God placed in us humans to keep us from self-destructing!

I was talking with our son Howie on the phone recently. He and I are constantly on the phone sharing our latest thoughts with one another. What he shared with me will explain in three words what I have spent hours writing about. He said, "Dad, life has its problems and we must learn how to deal with them. I have found that the solution to life's problems can be found in three basic steps: recover, regroup, and reload!" Thanks, Howie. Why didn't you call me sooner!

Personal Application: Prayerfully write down your answers to the following questions.

1. What emotional expression do you think Abraham and Sarah had when they laughed, mere astonishment or disbelief or both?

2. What reaction would you have had if God told you that you would be soon be doing something you never imagined you would do?

3. Considering what you know about this story, what are some of the challenges Abraham faced when Sara encouraged him to have a child with Hagar, her maid?

4. As you were growing up, how did you deal with disappointments, and surprises? Give an example of each. Was laughter a part of it?

Read Ahead (small group): Read Chapter 4: Keep Listening
The space below is provided to write any thoughts or insights you receive from Reading Chapter 4.

_____

_____

_____

Take this Survey
Ranking yourself from 1 to 10, how satisfied are you with your sense of humor?

1 being: "seldom laugh" and 10 being: "I laugh a lot." Circle one number.

1   2   3   4   5   6   7   8   9   10

Comments _____

_____

Essential References: Nehemiah 8:10; Job 8:21; Psalm 26:11; Psalm 37:13; Psalm 126:2; Ecclesiastes 3:4; Luke 6:21.

Chapter 4

Keep Listening

"God, who at various times and in various ways spoke in time past to the fathers by the prophets, has in these last days spoken to us by His Son, whom He has appointed heir of all things, through whom also He made the worlds; who being the brightness of His glory and the express image of His person and upholding all things by the word of His power, when He had by Himself purged your sins, sat down at the right hand of the Majesty on high." (Hebrews 1:1-3)

The Christian Herald [London] years ago told about a missionary who was looking for a word for obedience. One day he called for his dog and it came running to him. One of the natives said to the missionary in his language '*Mui adem delegan ge*, which means in free translation, "your dog is all ears." The missionary knew immediately that he had found the perfect word for obedience.

Jesus makes it clear in Revelation that listening is paramount to His relationship with His bride, the Church. Jesus presently sits at the right hand of the Father as mediator and communicates with His espoused Bride. The Church consists of every born-again believer who individually and personally can communicate with Christ through prayer. Prayer is not a one-way conversation. Christ's bride-to-be, the Church, prays and the espoused Groom [Jesus] speaks to the Church through the Scriptures and the Holy Spirit. The only difference between how Jesus spoke to the Church when He was on earth and how He communicates with the Church now is that He was physically there. And now, He exists on earth today in the embodiment of the Holy Spirit and God's written Word. Jesus communicated the entire book of Revelation to John the Beloved when John was exiled on the Isle of Patmos. Jesus said to the seven churches of Revelation, "He who has an ear, let him hear what the Spirit says to the churches." (Revelation 2:17) Even though we have physical ears, it doesn't mean we have good hearing. God has a voice and that voice is the Holy Spirit and His Word, the Bible.

I agree that He can speak in many other ways also, including signs and wonders, dreams and even in an audible voice [as He did to Samuel] (I Samuel 3:7-11) and Paul (Acts 9:1-19)], and others if He so desires. Those "other ways" that God speaks to us will never disagree with the written Word. The Bible confirms the fact that we are led by the Holy Spirit, "as many as are led by the Spirit of God they are the sons of God." (Romans 8:14) The more a person is led by the Spirit of God the more he will be "all ears" [obedient to God]. Also, "since the Greek word translated *led* is a present participle, it may be translated 'as many as are continually being led by the Spirit of God.' This leading is not to be restricted to objective knowledge of the commands of Scripture and conscious effort to obey them [though it most certainly includes that]. Rather, it more fully includes the subjective factor of being sensitive to the promptings of the Holy Spirit throughout the day, promptings that if genuinely from the Holy Spirit will never encourage us to act contrary to Scripture." (Romans 8:14)[28]

Furthermore, listening is more than just hearing; it also includes caring. Listening requires spending time with God expecting to hear from Him. Jesus sits at the highest position in heaven at the Father's right-hand interceding on our behalf. (Romans 8:34) Jesus must have prayed a lot when He was on earth because Luke says, "as He was praying in a certain place, when He ceased that one of His disciples said to Him, 'Lord teach us to pray, as John also taught his disciples.' So, He said to them, when you pray say: 'Our Father. . .'." (Luke 11:1). It is important to note that the disciples didn't ask Jesus to teach them to preach or even how to perform miracles, but how to pray. They saw in Jesus the need and benefit of prayer.

We hear from God:

- Through His Word (*logos*)
- Through the Holy Spirit (*rhema*)
- In dreams and visions
- Through signs and wonders, miracles
- Through gifts given in the Church: apostles, prophets, pastors, evangelists, and teachers (Ephesians 4: 11, 12)

God hears from us:

- When we pray and fast
- When we humble ourselves and repent
- When we praise and worship Him
- When we turn from wicked ways
- When we are being led by the Holy Spirit

Listening to God

There is a big difference between listening and actually hearing. Jesus said, "He who has ears to hear, let him hear!" This statement implies that it takes more than physical ears to hear the voice of God. To hear God, we must also have a soft heart. "Today, if you will hear His voice, harden not your hearts." (Hebrews 3:7-8)

Why We Don't Hear from God

Recently, Joy Behar, one of the hosts on *The View*, a national television program, insinuated that anyone who claimed that God spoke to them must have a mental problem. Her comments tell me that she has never heard God speak to her, and/or she was taught that God no longer speaks to people, or she has heard Him but won't acknowledge it. Some people believe that when we talk to God we're praying, but when God talks to us, we're schizophrenic.

Other Reasons Why
- If people claim to believe in God and don't hear from Him, maybe they are too busy to listen to God.
- They think too much of themselves, or they don't think they need to hear from God.
- They could be full of bitterness and unforgiveness and blame God for their problems.

Alan Lockerman, retired pastor of First Baptist Church, Cleveland, TN, lists in order of importance, four reasons why we don't hear from God:

1. Chaos (busyness)
2. Ego (the self is our greatest enemy)
3. Iniquity (sinning willfully)
4. Bitterness (blaming God for our misfortune)

> Don't say God isn't speaking to you when your Bible is closed.

A man from Leeds, England, visited a doctor to have his hearing checked. The doctor removed the man's hearing aid, and the patient's hearing immediately improved! He had been wearing the hearing aid in the wrong ear for over twenty years! The greatest struggle in life is not against Satan but against self. We are our own greatest enemy by far. If we are not hearing from God, it may be that we are not reading the Bible. If we will open our Bibles, the author will show up and talk with us through the Holy Spirit.

Satan doesn't have creative power, but he does have corrupted or perverted power. He distorts and dirties what God has created. This corruption dulls spiritual hearing. The dullness is more than wax in the ear; the spiritual ear is corrupted and, thus, the voice of God is tuned out. The ear becomes tuned to Satan's frequency. Here is an illustration that shows how one sound affects another and how listening to negative thoughts can result in living a negative life.

Two Sounds Become One

If you put two pianos in a room, and you hit a key on one of them, the same key on the other piano will resonate. It is called "sympathetic resonance" [vibration].[29] When God sent His Son into the world this is what happened. Jesus became human like us but was without sin. Spiritual sympathetic resonance happens when we become more like Christ once His presence enters our lives through the Holy Spirit. We are changed to become more like Him. "Let His mind be in you which was also in Jesus Christ." (Philippians 2:6) When we hurt, He hurts. Just as we are tempted, Jesus was also tempted but remained without sin. Whatever we are going through, God has already experienced it through His Son.

Listening and caring go together like two pieces of bread for a sandwich. The two pieces hold together all the in-between stuff. I saw this truth in action recently. It happened during dinner at a local restaurant. There were several of us who got together for dinner following Sunday morning church. I have learned that you can tell that people care by the way they listen to others. Seated across from me was a young man named Kaleb who was seated next to an elderly lady. She is in her mid-eighties and totally blind. She was in a talkative mood, so Kaleb mostly listened to her for over an hour. I watched him sit there patiently listening to her as if she were someone his own age.

Kaleb is not a stranger to me; I had performed his parent's wedding and had dedicated him to the Lord when he was born. I learned that he is studying for the ministry, and he and his wife plan to work in the children's ministry at his parents' church. As important as it is that we listen to each other, it is even more important that we listen to God's voice.

There are three characters in the Bible who bless me when I think about them and how they listened to God and how the Holy Spirit was part of their ministry. They are Gideon, Elisha, and Amasai. (I Chronicles 12:18) All three men were "clothed with the Holy Spirit."

The story of Gideon is found in the book of Judges. Israel was under God's punishment by the Midianites for seven years for their sin of idolatry. God called Gideon with the words: "The Lord is with you, you mighty man of valor." (Judges 6:12b) Gideon must have been puzzled by the angel calling him a "mighty man of valor" since at the time he "threshed wheat in the winepress, in order to hide it from the Midianites."(v. 11b) Gideon sought a sign from God to prove that it was God talking to him. God appeased Gideon by asking him to put a meat offering of a young goat and unleavened bread under a tree. An angel of the Lord put out his staff and touched the offering and a fire came out of the rock and consumed the offering. As a result, Gideon built an altar there to the Lord.

Things began to accelerate. That same night the Lord tells Gideon to tear down the altar and idols of Baal that his father used, and then he was to build an altar out of the idols and offer a young bull as a sacrifice. Gideon took ten men with him the next night because he feared his father and did as God commanded. The cult of the Canaanite goddess Asherah was not pleased to say the least. War was on. The point I want to emphasize is the following: "But the Spirit of the Lord came upon Gideon; then he blew the trumpet, and the Abiezites gathered behind him." (v. 34). In Hebrew this literally means: "The Spirit of the Lord clothed Himself with Gideon."[30]

> With God's help you are amazing. Remember that!

When I speak about Gideon, I visually illustrate what happens when the Spirit clothed Gideon and Amasai. I take my coat off and I hold the limp lifeless coat in my hand and say, "This is me; like the coat I am powerless to do anything." Then I put one arm in a sleeve and point out how that I represent the Holy Spirit clothing me with Himself. The sleeve can move, but only with the arm's [the Holy Spirit] assistance. I then put the coat on to show the coat's [our] ability to move under the influence [the Holy Spirit] of whoever is wearing it. This is what Paul meant when he said, "I can do all things, through Christ who strengthens me." (Philippians 4:13)

Music to My Ears

The other Biblical characters are Elisha, a prophet of Israel, and Amasai a commander of King David's Judean army. Amasai and his men came to meet David who then invited Amasai to join him. That is when the Spirit came upon Amasai, chief of the captains, who said: "We are yours, O David; We are on your side, O son of Jesse! Peace, Peace to you, and peace to your helpers! For your God helps you." (I Chronicles 12:18)

Let's consider Elisha. When Jehoshaphat was at war, his army marched into a desert place with no water. Through the help of the prophet Elisha, the Lord provided water. To celebrate the miracle, Elisha called for the musicians. When the musicians played, the hand of the Lord came upon Elisha, and he said, "Thus says the Lord: Make this valley full of ditches." (2 Kings 3:15b-16). The same thing happened to Elisha that happened to Gideon and Amasai; the Spirit of the Lord clothed Himself with them.

Gideon and Elisha were men who were victorious over their enemies through the power of the Holy Spirit. Music and musical instruments were used by God to anoint prophets to prophesy against His enemies; trumpets were used to bring down the walls of Jericho, and David's harp subdued demons. The example of hitting a key on a piano and the same sound resonating on another piano in the room is the same principle when music was played in the above cases. When music was played, it brought the sound and the presence of the Holy Spirit together. This shows that music can play a major role to clear the atmosphere of outside interference so that prayer and listening to God work together more effectively. Amasai was not assisted with music or musical instruments, yet he was clothed with the same Holy Spirit that Gideon and Elisha were, and he received discernment from the Holy Spirit to join David's army.

Beauty for Ashes
It is virtually impossible to listen to God when we worry. Five basic fears that hinder our ability to listen are a fear of poverty, fear of criticism, fear of ill health, fear of aging, and the fear of death. These fears can block out the voice of God. In fact, fear prevents worship. So, how do we deal with it? We pray! Prayer will lead us through the door of faith into the very presence of God. Worry will lead us in the opposite direction. Paul's advice to Timothy is worth repeating: "For God has not given us a Spirit of fear, but of power and of love and of a sound mind." (2 Timothy 1:7). Discipline yourself to pray, to talk to God, then stop and listen for the Holy Spirit to answer. If prayer doesn't cancel our fear, fear will cancel our prayer. We can't worry and worship.

> You have a house inside of you
> where you can fight your battles through.
> And God will tell you what to do,
> and make your heart both strong and true.
> Anonymous

Author Margaret Eggleston, in one of her books, tells about a janitor who was sweeping the floor of a bank. There on the floor was a stack of bills under the desk hidden beneath some wastepaper. He thought he could certainly use the money and took it. He went home, and about an hour later he brought the money back and put it on the desk of the president. The next day when the president asked him if he was the one who put the money on the desk, he said, "Yes." The president asked, "Why? We could never have proven that you were the one who took the money." The man said, "I could have kept the money, but I have to live with myself, and I don't want to live with a thief."[31] Because he was attuned to God, the Holy Spirit convicted him to do the right thing.

Sharing and Praising

Sharing

There isn't much that I can do, but I can share my bread with you, and sometimes share a sorrow, too—as on our way we go.

There isn't much that I can do, but I can sit an hour with you, and I can share a joke with you, and sometimes share reverses, too—as on our way we go.

There isn't much that I can do, but I can share my flowers with you, and I can share my books with you and sometimes share your burdens too—as on our way we go.

There isn't much that I can do, but I can share my songs with you, and I can share my mirth with you, and sometimes come and laugh with you—as on our way we go.

There isn't much that I can do, but I can share my hopes with you, and I can share my fears with you, and sometimes shed some tears with you—as on our way we go.

There isn't much that I can do, but I can share my friends with you, and I can share my life with you, and oftentimes share a prayer with you—as on our way we go. (Anonymous)

Praising

"Let them praise His name with the dance." Psalm 149:5
"Praise Him with the timbral and dance. Psalm 150:4.

Embracing the Future

Habakkuk lived in one of the most critical periods of Judah's history. Israel had been captured by the Assyrians in 722 BC, and Assyria was breathing down the neck of Judah. Babylon was rising as a major threat and would eventually capture Judah in 586 BC. All around Judah was war much like what is happening in the Middle East right now. King Josiah's reform was a thing of the past and Judah's spirituality was in free-fall, similar to what America and the world as a whole are experiencing today.

At first, Habakkuk struggled with the bad things going on around him. His mind was overwhelmed with the evil that his people were doing. Where is God, he asks? Evil men are in control of everything. He couldn't see God anywhere. Don't we feel this way sometimes? We feel the threat of nuclear war; children are gassed to death in Syria; school children are being massacred in their classrooms; women are being raped; gangs are committing drive-by shootings; airplanes are flying into high-rise buildings killing thousands; shopping malls are being attacked by terrorists, and we all face the threat of world economic collapse. Leaders are powerless to prevent it. And it will get worse. Violence and terror were what Habakkuk was seeing and hearing. Things were terrible; he saw worse things coming for Judah, and it was just on the horizon. But then he heard God say, "Hold on, all is not lost."

> You will never do God's will living in the past.

Habakkuk's first three verses in Chapter 1 are nothing like what he writes in Chapter 3:17-19. Everything has turned 180 degrees. He dances on the rubble! He's not worried any more about the circumstances. He looks toward heaven for an answer. He stops looking at the problem and looks at the problem solver. That is exactly what we should do when we are overwhelmed by Satan. We don't focus on the problem; we focus on the power of God. Paul writes in Ephesians 3:20, "Now unto Him who is able to do exceeding, abundantly, above all we can ask or think, according to the power that works in us."

Nehemiah is another example of a great leader who listened to God and was determined to override the circumstances and dance on the rubble. Before he laid one stone, he did what I like to think of as an act of worship and thanksgiving that we often forget. He showed gratitude for answered prayer. The narrative is found in Nehemiah 2:12-18. The prophet rode on horseback in the moonlight around the ruins of

Jerusalem. I imagine him thanking God for answered prayer at each of the eight gates of the city, getting down off his horse at some point and doing a Jewish victory dance on the rubble of broken-down walls, gates, and charred pillars. Certainly, his spirit danced within him. Sometimes we need to be alone with God so that we can be free to worship and listen to God as we please and as it pleases Him.

God Listens to Us

God hears our prayers, but He also hears our complaints. A good example comes from Adrian Rogers. He is a former pastor of First Baptist Church in Memphis, Tennessee, who told of a time during his first years of ministry when he and his family planned to drive to the west coast for a vacation. Their vacation plan was to eat a meal by the ocean. Their son was young, and when they arrived and went to the restaurant, they were shocked that the prices were so high. Still, they decided to spend the money since they had driven so far. When their food arrived, their son began to cry, and Pastor Rogers asked him what was wrong. He replied, "They put beet juice on my mashed potatoes." Pastor Rogers explained how some Christians complain over the smallest thing when they are seated at the table of Christ and have everything to praise God for.

There is a warning in the Old Testament that will make us think twice before we complain about anything again, including beet juice on our mashed potatoes. It is found in Deuteronomy 28:47-48: "Because you did not serve the Lord your God with joy and gladness of heart, for the abundance of everything, therefore you shall serve your enemies, whom the Lord will send against you, in hunger, in thirst, in nakedness and in need of everything; and He will put a yoke of iron on your neck until He has destroyed you."

God promises us four things in this life: peace, power, purpose, and tribulation. We have little or no problem accepting the promised peace, power, and purpose in our lives. But we don't want to accept the tribulation [such as stress, pressure, and oppression] that is also promised. We know, though, that with our faith in Jesus Christ we can be overcomers. He said in John 16:33 to "be of good cheer for I have overcome the world."

In his book, *The Circle Maker*, Mark Batterson makes the following statement, "Lord, you can't do anything but answer our prayer if we believe you." It is impossible for God not to keep His Word. The problem lies in our failure to believe what God says. The Bible simply says, "What father, if his son asks for bread will give him a stone? Or if he asks for a fish, will give him a serpent? If you being evil know how to give good gifts to your children, how much more will your heavenly father give good things to them who ask him?" (Matthew 7:9-11). Kaye and I have kept this verse foremost in our memories. When we see the numbers 7:11 anywhere, they serve as a reminder of this Scripture at which time we pause and praise God and His faithfulness. We have even had our bill at a restaurant total $7.11. It is impossible for God not to keep His promises to us. That's what God loves to do. Believe that!

Results of God Listening to Us
King David believed that God listened to his prayers. He wrote, "The eyes of the Lord are on the righteous. And His ears are open to their cry. The righteous cry out, and the Lord hears." (Psalm 34:15,17) [Note of interest: more writers in the New Testament quoted Psalm 34 than any other.] God is a prayer-hearing God. Habakkuk summed up his faith in God listening to him in 3:17-19. "Although the fig tree shall not blossom, neither shall fruit be in the vines; the labor of the olive shall fail, and the fields shall yield no meat; the flock shall be cut off from the fold, and there shall be no herd in the stalls: Yet I will rejoice in the Lord, I will joy in the God of my salvation. The Lord God is my strength and he will make my feet like hinds' feet, and he will make me to walk upon mine high places. To the chief singer on my stringed instruments." You talk about someone dancing on the rubble, David and Habakkuk danced on the rubble despite their circumstances.

Habakkuk discovered that God listened to him when he prayed. When we are on higher ground we can see further because we are on top of the problem. David's feet became as deer's feet able to overcome the greatest problems he faced. David went from doubt to faith. Faith in God is where joy is born. He stopped looking at men for solutions and looked to God. He went from Death Valley to Mt. Everest in one giant leap. He even makes the statement, "The just shall live by his faith." (2:4) Wow! What a turn around.

Listening and Believing/Believing and Seeing

In 1880, Helen Keller was born into a well-off Alabama family. When she was nineteen months old, Helen became seriously ill and was left deaf and blind. At the age of six, she was referred to Alexander Graham Bell who at the time was working with deaf children. He couldn't help her, so he referred her to The Perkins Institute for the Blind. It was there that she met Annie Sullivan who was a 20-year-old graduate of the school and partially blind herself. Annie and Helen became friends, and Annie asked for permission to take Helen away from her family to help her concentrate and learn. Helen's family agreed.

The rest is history. Helen went on to become the first blind person ever to graduate from college. In 1915, she founded Helen Keller International, a nonprofit organization for the prevention of blindness. She also helped to create the American Civil Liberties Union (ACLU). Helen wrote twelve books. She met every president from Grover Cleveland to Lyndon B. Johnson. She lived a full and productive life for eighty-seven years, dying in 1968. One of her notable sayings is, "What is worse than blindness is to have eyes and not be able to see. What is equally worse than deafness is to have ears and not be able to hear God speak to you." She also said, "The marvelous richness of human experience would lose something of rewarding joy if there were no limitations to overcome."[32] The hilltop hour would not be half so wonderful if there were no dark valleys to traverse. Helen danced on the rubble despite being deaf and blind.

How God Speaks

God speaks to us through nature. One morning I was awakened to the sweet song of a little bird singing outside my window. The song inspired me to write a poem entitled *Heavenly Messenger*. [You will find the poem in the Poetry section.] God never stops speaking, and we should never stop listening.

When we lived in Jackson, Mississippi, I enrolled in a Greek class at Mississippi College. One day I came across a verse in the Bible that puzzled me. The verse was Hebrews 13:5b: "For He Himself has said, I will never leave you nor forsake you." I noticed that the word "never" [a negative] in the complete verse was repeated five times. I was just beginning to learn Greek, so I didn't know that to emphasize something, the Greeks would repeat a word. In this case, there were five "negatives" [nevers].

I immediately called my Greek professor and asked him what these strange groupings of negatives meant. And he said to me, "Roy, God wants you to know that He will never, never, never, never, never, leave you nor forsake you." His clarification of that Scripture has meant the world to me over the years. What our heavenly Father is simply saying is "I will never forsake you or leave you without support." And that is true, but I think there is also a deeper meaning. What I'm about to share with you is not Greek grammar, but a spark which these "negatives" lit in my spirit and blessed me. Grammatically, these five "nevers" are considered negatives in the Greek language but, I see them, not as negatives but as "positives."

The results of five "negatives" is five positives declaring that God will never leave us or forsake us. God's "nevers" are always "positives." God's "no's" always result in a positive outcome. God's "no" to Paul's request to remove the thorn from his flesh was for Paul's good and Paul accepted it. The Scripture says, "And we know that ALL things work together for good to those who love God, to those who are the called according to His purpose." (Romans 8:28)

Our Heavenly Father is never "negative" toward us but is always "positive" regarding every detail of our lives. If only we can always see that God's "no's" are "yeses." Because of this, we can totally rely on His will in every circumstance that we face. We can accept our Heavenly Father's "no" with greater assurance that the "no" will work a "positive" result in us, even if we never see it in this life. That is what we call trust. Jesus, knowing this, prayed: "Not my will but thine be done." (Luke 22:42) Jesus knew that His Father was stage-managing every move of His life. Isn't that wonderful? With that assurance, we all should be able to dance on the rubble.

A loving parent doesn't say "no" to his children expecting "negative" results. It is intended for their good. A child will not always understand why his father or mother says "no" to him playing in a busy street. Not until he matures into an adult.

Our son, Howie, is the pastor of City Gate Church in Gallatin, Tennessee, and is very familiar with the verse Hebrews 13:5b. He called and shared Isaiah 41:10 with me. It says, "Fear thou not; for I am with you; be not dismayed, for I am thy God. I will strengthen you. Yes, I will help you, I will uphold you with my righteousness right hand." Howie pointed out to me that the verse has five I am's, and I will's that matched the five "nevers" in Hebrews 13:5b.

> Life has an "if" in the center of it.

What Happens When God Hears
Life plans change constantly and what better way to face the changes in life than to trust God with our plans. My outlook on life is to write my plans in pencil and give God the eraser. It works! Sometimes you need to dance it out! And if you stumble, make it a part of the dance. Life has an "if" in the center of it. "Ifs" are necessary in life. Life comes with conditions attached to it. The "If" is like a flashing sign ahead that says, "Your life is not on autopilot; you must make choices and "If" you make the right ones, with God's help, you will be blessed. "If" you don't, life will be more than a trial or two. After I pray, I close with the affirmation: "If it's the Lord's will."

I discovered the following declaration on the back of the "pencil art" Keagan Kennedy, my great niece, made for me. It says: "I may not have gone where I intended to go, but I think I have ended up where I intended to be." The front side says: "Everything happens for a reason." Thanks Keagan; you are a blessing.

> Make your plans, write them in pencil, and give God the eraser.

A Fresh Perspective
Listening to God can help us gain a fresh perspective. We can become so familiar with God that we can barely recognize Him. Yes, blindness is a physical issue, but it can also be a spiritual issue. Consider the poor blind man who held a cardboard sign with the words: "I am blind. Please help!" scribbled on it. He sat on the street corner with the sign and a tin cup to collect change from passersby. Every now and then, someone

would drop some change into the cup, and he would thank them. But it amounted to so little. One day, a man stopped, dropped some coins in his cup, and asked if he could have a look at his sign. The blind man was happy to oblige. The stranger held the sign and wrote something on it and handed it back to the blind man. It wasn't very long after the stranger left that a lot more people stopped and gave money to the blind man. He was puzzled by this until he heard a familiar voice. It was the stranger who had come by earlier and asked to look at his sign. The blind man explained to the stranger that since he had left him, people had filled his cup with money. He couldn't understand why.

The stranger explained that when he read the sign it said, "I'm blind. Please help." He went on to explain that he wrote additional words below. The blind man asked the stranger what he had written on his sign. He said: "I wrote: It's a beautiful day, but I cannot see it." The added words written by the stranger touched the hearts of the people to give more generously to the blind man because, despite his blindness, he accentuated the positive and put the beautiful day first and his blindness second.

Those who know me, ask me all the time, "How do you feel physically?" and I tell them that I only have two kinds of days: good ones and better ones. I know what they expect me to say: good ones and bad ones. They are surprised at my answer. I can't tell you how many times people respond with the comment that my optimistic response has helped them to think more positively about their situation or problem. Every moment of every day is precious, and we need to seize every second with gratitude. Do we have a bad day sometimes? Yes, but we don't have to put it on a billboard and advertise it.

Listening Is Hard Sometimes

Sometime things go wrong, and we all tend to focus on the pain more than the pleasure. I confess that it is not easy to choose the high road of thanksgiving, but it is the will of God for us. I am by no means implying that we should never shed tears, acknowledge the pain, or tell the truth about how we feel, but I am saying that the negative things should not be our main concern and focus in life. Sometimes it takes God to open our spiritual eyes so that we can see the positive

Life holds many challenges. How we respond to them is important. I have found that my attitude toward a situation makes all the difference in the world. Dan Green in his book: *Finish Strong, More Than a statement...It's an Attitude*, nailed it. He wrote, "Regardless of what came before or of what is yet to come, what matters most right now is how I choose to respond to the challenge before me. Will I lie down, or will I fight? The choice is mine, and I choose to finish strong."

> If you have a pulse, you have a purpose.

Another one of my favorite Scriptures consists of the last two verses (24, 25) of the book of Jude: "Now unto Him who is able to keep you from falling [stumbling] and to present you faultless, before the presence of His glory with exceeding joy. To the only wise God, our Savior, be glory, and majesty, dominion and power, both now and ever." I cherish the part that says, "Now unto him who is able to keep you from falling." It's not we who are able to deal with pain and tragedies in life, but it is HE who makes us able. This is a promise to each of us who desire by the Grace of God to finish strong. If we will just listen to God and realize that If Jesus did it all, what more can we do?"

Trusting is Hard Sometimes
I woke up early this morning thinking about a story I had read years ago of a woman missionary who was captured by the Japanese during World War II. She and her husband were missionaries in the Philippines. She was imprisoned and her husband was taken away to a separate concentration camp; she never heard from him again. I wish I could recall the name of the book, but I do remember her name was Rose.

Rose was taken to more than one concentration camp in the Philippines, but the story I am sharing happened while at the last camp. She was put in a cell with only a small window higher than her head. Rose could climb up on a piece of furniture and look out, which she did often. Her food consisted of a weak broth with a small piece of bread that was usually hard and moldy. One day she was thrilled to see what she thought was rice floating on top of her broth, but it turned out to be maggots. She ate it and was glad to get the protein. Rose's health began to decline drastically. Plagued with dysentery, dehydration, and near-death, Rose was barely hanging on to life.

One day while she was looking out of her window, Rose saw a person's hand come out of the hedges with a banana in it. A woman prisoner inside the camp reached through the prison wire fence and took the banana. Someone from outside of the prison was feeding someone they knew inside. Rose thought of how wonderful it would be to have a banana. But she reasoned that it would be impossible to get a banana inside the prison cell. She even said that to God in her prayers. Rose was in for the surprise of her life.

Shortly after this, Rose was visited by a Japanese officer who was there on a visit from another camp. It so happened that he was from one of the previous camps she had been held in. When he came to her prison cell, she recognized him because he had been kind to her. Later, after he had left, she realized that she had failed to bow in his presence which was a punishable offense. Apparently, the carelessness on Rose's part didn't matter to him because he was more interested in her welfare. He recognized that Rose was in poor health and was badly malnourished. After a brief visit, the officer left.

He returned with a stalk of bananas for Rose. She was stunned at the gift. Remember, she had said to God that she knew it would be impossible for Him to get even one banana into her prison cell. Rose thanked the officer through tears of gratitude, and he left. She put the bananas in an opposite corner of her cell and refused to touch one of them for a long time. She was overwhelmed with guilt for not believing that God could provide her with one banana. Later when she could bring herself to eat one, Rose counted them and, if I remember correctly, there were ninety or more bananas on the stalk. Rose was released from prison and came to America with her testimony of God's faithfulness. I don't know if she is still alive, or with Jesus, but I believe Rose danced on her rubble.

Speak the Truth
Listen to what God said to one of Job's friends, Eliphaz the Temanite, this was following Job's test: God said, "My wrath is kindled against thee, and against thy two friends: for ye have not spoken of me the thing that is right, as my servant Job hath." (Job 42:7) And God repeats the phrase in verse 8: "for ye have not spoken of me the thing that is

right, like my servant Job."

Rose made the mistake of not trusting that God could give her one banana. She did not speak through faith. God said to Abraham, "Is there anything too hard for me?" (Genesis 18:14) God is omnipotent. He is all powerful. Therefore, to say that God can't do something is to "speak of Him the thing that is not right." (Jeremiah 32:27) The friends of Job got into trouble with God for the same reason; they misquoted or spoke words that were not God's truth.

It is wrong for us to say, "Thus says God . . ." or to say, "God says . . . thus and so." If God didn't say it, or give us permission to say it, don't say it. It is just as wrong to say, "God can't do this or that." What is impossible with humans is possible with God. We should not put words into God's mouth or presume to know what He would say. Hebrews 10:23 says, "Let us hold fast our profession of faith, without wavering for He is faithful who has promised." We must say it the way God says it, the way His Word says it. We must agree with the Word of God without wavering.

Trust and Obey

The Philippines were hit by a typhoon that killed thousands. One person commented, "God must have been somewhere else." God is never somewhere else because He is Omnipresent. [Jehovah-*SHAMMAH*, "God is always there"]. When disaster hits, it seems to us that He is not there. And in those times, we are tempted to say what is not true about God. God loves us, and He will never leave us or forsake us, not in our worst trial. He weeps along with us when we suffer. God didn't cause the typhoon, the Adversary did. God didn't cause the sickness and loss of everything in Job's case either.

God will reward those who say it like He says it, but He will also rebuke those who do not say it like He says it. Job's friends can attest to that. Job was rewarded for saying it like God said it, "So the Lord blessed the latter end of Job more than his beginning." (Job 42:12a) As for Job's friends who were required by God to make animal sacrifices; they humbled themselves and asked Job to pray for them. Job had to have a forgiving spirit too. His sickness was not reversed until he prayed for his friends who had done him wrong. "And the Lord turned the captivity [sickness] of Job, when he prayed for his friends: also, the Lord gave Job twice as much as he had before." (Job 42:10)

Obedience and trust can be measured and rewarded. In Job's case, it was measured by his willingness to trust God, to forgive and pray for his enemies. His reward was prosperity, family, and spiritual insight. He said, "I have heard of You by the hearing of the ear, but now my eyes see You. Therefore, I abhor myself, and repent in dust and ashes." (Job 42:5) "We have heard with our ears, O God." (Psalm 44:1) Obedience, in Israel's case [Joshua], can be measured in that they only conquered one-third of the enemy's territory that God promised to them. He said to Joshua, "Every place that the sole of your feet will tread upon I have given to you, as I said to Moses." (Joshua 1:3)

When we are going through a trial there is nothing better to do than read the Bible and listen for the Holy Spirit to speak to us. Whatever the Bible and the Holy Spirit say, then we "say it like God says it." Repeat the Word of God over and over just like the Bible says it. One of the Scriptures I like to say over and over is Psalm 23. It is amazing how reading and repeating the Word of God can build one's faith. Read and digest Scripture slowly. The Scripture says, "faith comes by hearing, and hearing by the Word of God." (Romans 10:17) We must listen to God, stand in faith, and say it like God says it. Try it. It works.

Responding to God's Voice

Praising and rejoicing are music to our heavenly Father's ears. We direct our praise toward God, and that praise returns to us in abundant blessings. Kaye and I joined our daughter Karen and son-in-law Huey at the Big River Grill in Chattanooga, Tennessee, to celebrate our daughter's birthday. Our server was a young lady named Mary. She graduated from college with a degree in music and was going back to school to earn a master's degree in education. Her reason for changing her major was because she couldn't find employment in the music field. I said to Mary, "Your interest in music reminds me of prayer being like music, the rests are just as important as the notes." Prayer is like that in that God's silence, or "no," to our prayers is just as important as when He answers "yes" to them."

Mary told us that when she first enrolled in music class, she was taught that the definition of music was a combination of silence, listening, and sound. I had never heard that definition of music before, but it is a perfect definition of prayer. Sometimes God speaks and sometimes He is silent; put the two together and they make perfect harmony. When we pray, our prayers are music to our Heavenly Father's ears. (Philippians 4:6-7)

We know God isn't ignoring us when He is silent; He is listening to us and will speak to our need at the appropriate time. Understanding this simple truth will make it possible to dance on the rubble in spite of the silence because ". . . we know that all things [both the silence and the sound] work together for good to them that love God, to them who are the called according to His purpose." (Romans 8:28)

Whether our need is an immediate one, or a need we have lived with for years, don't give up. Christ is the answer. He alone can make up for our lack of faith. Pour out your heart to Him because "The eyes of the Lord are upon the righteous and His ears are open to their cries." (Psalm 34:15) When we've prayed until we can't pray anymore, maybe it is time to change our approach and do just the opposite. Take a pause from asking and start praising! Alan Lockerman, retired pastor of First Baptist Church, Cleveland, Tennessee, defines faith this way: "Faith is a conscious state of dependence on God."

Prayer is always appropriate, but sometimes we need to stop asking and start praising as Habakkuk did. Sometimes we don't have a choice. We pray, ask, knock and seek, but there is no immediate answer. What do we do then? We break out into a praise! David knew to praise God in his time of discouragement. He expresses his thankfulness for God turning his mourning into dancing. "You have turned for me my mourning into dancing; you have put off my sackcloth and clothed me with gladness, to the end that my glory may sing praise to You and not be silent. O Lord my God, I will give thanks to You forever." (Psalm 30:11-12)

I don't think we Christians know how blessed we are. Just think, we have what I call triple coverage: the blood, the angels, and the Holy Spirit. The blood purchased our salvation; therefore, we have that security. The angels are encamped around us for our physical protection, and we are filled with the Holy Spirit who is our teacher, guide, and power source to help us overcome and to share the Gospel with others.

God is amazing! He is willing to do everything to help us human beings connect with him including signs and wonders to build our faith. In the Old Testament, one way humans connected with the presence of God was with the construction of Solomon's Temple. When Solomon built the temple, furnishings were brought in, including the Ark of the Covenant. "Then the priest brought in the ark of the covenant of the Lord to its place, into the inner sanctuary of the temple, to the Most Holy Place, under the wings of the cherubim. For the cherubim spread their two wings over the place of the Ark, and the cherubim overshadowed the Ark and its poles. The poles extended so that the ends of the poles could be seen from the holy place, in front of the inner sanctuary, but they could not be seen from outside. And they are there to this day." (I Kings 8:6-8)

Notice how the description of the poles of the Ark of the Covenant were "extended so that the ends of the poles could be seen from the holy place." Why? To assure the priest of Jehovah's presence. Only the High Priest could go into the "Most Holy Place" once a year to put blood on the mercy seat located on the lid of the Ark of the Covenant, between the two cherubim. Therefore, the two poles used to carry the ark by four men, were positioned so that the impression of the pole's ends pushed against the curtain that divided the Most Holy Place from the Holy Place could be seen. The poles couldn't be seen, just the impression of the ends of the poles. The Ark of the Covenant represented the presence of God while the extended poles represented physical proof and reassurance of God's presence to the priests.

God is always willing to meet us half-way in our search for Him. God said to Jeremiah, "Then you will call upon Me and go and pray to Me, and I will listen to you. And you will seek Me and find Me, when you search for Me with all your heart." (Jeremiah 29:13-14) God is always willing to do whatever it takes to increase our faith so that our prayers can be answered. The Bible is filled with examples of this: Gideon and the fleece, Moses and the burning bush, dividing of the Red Sea, David, Joshua and others. To nurture their faith God gave them tangible signs.

A Word of Caution

The Word of God and the Holy Spirit are our final authority and guide. Therefore, be careful about how much you rely on signs and wonders to guide you. God can get our attention in many ways, but He rarely uses anything other than the Scriptures and the Holy Spirit. God used a donkey one time to warn Balaam (Numbers 22:21-39), but you shouldn't worship the donkey.

Think about this. Anything you rely upon for spiritual guidance, other than Scripture and the Holy Spirit, will demand your loyalty and praise. God is Omnipresent [everywhere], Omniscient [all knowing], and Omnipotent [all powerful]. Stay close to Him and listen to Him through Scripture and the Holy Spirit. Just be cautious about seeking guidance from any source other than the Word of God. Keep your eyes and ears open and stay close to the Good Shepherd. There is an old saying that goes, "The closer you are to the shepherd, the safer you are from the wolves."

Your walk talks,
Your talk talks, but
Your walk talks more,
than your talk talks.

Mark Trummell

Study Guide: Keep Listening

Key Quote(s):

"He who has an ear, let him hear what the Spirit says to the churches." (Revelation 2:17)

"Listen contains the same letters as the word silent." Alferd Brendel

"I cannot hear what you say for listening to what you are." Ralph Waldo Emerson

"Listening is often the only thing needed to help someone." Anonymous

"Wisdom is the reward you get for a lifetime of listening when you would have rather talked." Mark Twain

Begin with Prayer

O, Lord give ear to my prayer today. I submit my ears to You. Speak to me through Your Holy Spirit. Help me to be a doer of Your spoken and written words and not a hearer only. Day and night, I long to hear Your voice. Save me, O God by your Son's name, Jesus, from the deception of religion. The enemy has prepared a net for me. Deliver me from my enemies. Defend me from those who plot against me. They are set to destroy me at no fault of mine. I trust You, O God, to be my defense and my refuge. As I wait upon Your guidance, as I wait upon Your voice to guide me, I will sing of Your power and Your mercy and keep on listening. In the name of Jesus. Amen.

Book: I Samuel

Author: Uncertain. However, Samuel could have written it or supplied the information.

Date: Between 931 BC and probably before 722 BC

Inspiration:

I Samuel 17:42, 43; 45-51

⁴² And when the Philistine looked about and saw David, he disdained him; for he was only a youth, ruddy and good-looking.

⁴³ So the Philistine said to David, "Am I a dog, that you come to me with sticks?" And the Philistine cursed David by his Gods.

⁴⁵ Then David said to the Philistine [Goliath], you come to me with a sword, a spear, and with a javelin. But I come to you in the name of the Lord of hosts, the God of the armies of Israel, whom you have defied.

⁴⁶ This day the Lord will deliver you into my hands, and I will strike you and take your head from you. And this day I will give the carcasses of the camp of the Philistines to the birds of the air and the wild beasts of the earth, that all the earth may know that there is a God in Israel.

⁴⁷ Then all this assembly shall know that the Lord does not save with sword and spear; for the battle is the Lord's, and He will give you into our hands.

⁴⁸ So it was, when the Philistine arose and came and drew near to meet David, that David hurried and ran toward the army to meet the Philistine.

⁴⁹ Then David put his hand in his bag and took out a stone; and he slung it and struck the Philistine in his forehead, so that the stone sank into his forehead, and he fell on his face to the earth.

⁵⁰ So David prevailed over the Philistine with a sling and a stone and struck the Philistine and killed him. But there was no sword in the hand of David.

⁵¹ Therefore David ran and stood over the Philistine, took his sword and drew it out of its sheath and killed him, and cut off his head with it. And when the Philistines saw that their champion was dead, they fled.

I Samuel 18:5-7

⁵ So David went out wherever Saul sent him and behaved wisely. And Saul set him over the men of war, and he was accepted in the sight of all the people and also in the sight of Saul's servants.

⁶ Now it had happened as they were coming home, when David was returning from the slaughter of the Philistine, that the women had come out of all the cities of Israel, singing and dancing, to meet King Saul, with tambourines, with joy, and with musical instruments.

⁷ So the women sang as they danced, and said: "Saul has slain his thousands, And David his ten thousand."

Backstory

David talked to God a lot and David listened to God a lot, but not always. And when he didn't listen, he got into trouble and had to repent. Yet, with David's many failures, God called him a man after His own heart. Why? I believe it was because David repented, loved, and listened to God. David was compliant, yielding, submissive, and obedient to Him.

David was about fifteen-years-old when Samuel anointed him King of Judah. David is described physically as being ruddy, with bright eyes, and good-looking. God said to Samuel: "'Arise, anoint him for this is the one!' Then Samuel took the horn of oil and anointed him in the midst of his brethren, and the Spirit of the Lord came upon David from that day forward. So, Samuel arose and went to Ramah." (I Samuel 15:12, 13)

David was known to seek God and to listen to Him. The many Psalms of David bear this out. In 1 Samuel 23:2,4, David sought guidance from the Lord. "Therefore, David inquired of the Lord, saying 'shall I go and attack the Philistines?' And the Lord said to David, 'Go and attack the Philistines and save Keilah.' David's men were afraid to go with him. So, the Bible says, "Then David inquired of the Lord once again. And the Lord answered him and said. 'Arise and go down to Keilah for I will deliver the Philistines into your hand.'" In the first thirteen verses of Chapter 23, David prays at least five times to the Lord for guidance. David listened to God and escaped a plot by Saul to kill him at Keilah.

Most of the individuals in the biblical stories that we read about in the Old Testament, as well as the New Testament, sought God for guidance in their work for Him. However, hearing from God and learning to listen to Him is not confined to biblical times. Seeking God's ear and then listening to his response is just as necessary in modern times. Just be very careful not to confuse superstition with the voice of the Holy Spirit. The Scriptures bear out the fact that the Holy Spirit and the Word of God are to be our ultimate sources for guidance. Furthermore, prayer is a direct means by which to communicate with God and for Him to communicate with us. It is one thing to talk to God, but then we must take time to listen for His answers. I believe we can talk to God and then we can articulate what God's response is to us.

I was in a "Break the 200 Barrier" seminar sponsored by John Maxwell and held in Marietta, Georgia. I went specially to hear John Maxwell speak, but when I learned that he was not going to speak that afternoon at 3:00 p.m., due to a previous engagement, I was ready to leave. After discussing the pros and cons of staying or leaving with the person accompanying me, we decided to stay for the 3:00 o'clock session. I had written off the possibility of anything good happening, but did I get an ear full [pun intended]!

The instructor stopped teaching at 3:55 and said to the group, "It is five minutes to 4:00 p.m., and I want you to pray and ask God this question: "Lord, what do You want to be in Your Church?" Usually when we call for the congregation to pray in my church, we pray with no time limit. I was honestly frustrated, and I thought, "What can God say in five minutes?" My experience regarding prayer was to pray long, extended prayers. I felt limiting God to a five minute one was insulting to Him.

Nevertheless, I bowed my head and prayed a feeble prayer saying, "God what do You want to be in Your Church?" Immediately, I heard God's voice in my spirit. He said, "I want to be . . ." and one by one I wrote down, in order, the four things He said to me that He wants to be:

- glorified
- known
- seen
- God

Not only was I was surprised with His immediate answer, I was also stunned by what God said. Hearing God is often easier than obeying him. James says, "Be doers of the word, and not hearers only, deceiving yourselves." (James 1:22) We have a compulsion to make up, or substitute, religion for obedience to the Word of God. There is a big difference between hearing God and listening to God. The latter requires patience and obedience.

David was a man after God's own heart. But what does that mean? It means in all our ways we should be in agreement with God. David yielded his will to God's will. He was compliant; that is, he was obedient and submissive to God.

Be careful when you ask God to speak to you about something

because He may ask you to do something you don't want to do. Remember this, God's written Word is not debatable. The way in which God speaks to us, whether through a dream, vision, or out of the written Word, He is to be obeyed. To not obey God's word is to reject God Himself. It is always wise to compare what you believe God is saying to you with what the Bible says. Also consider talking it through with someone whom you trust and respect.

No absolutes! Really?

I attended a seminar recently, and one of the statements that the instructor made was, "There is no such thing as an absolute." Then she began to criticize how confused Christians are who believe in an absolute God. She tried to prove that there are no absolutes by her absolute emphatic statement when she said, "There are no such things as absolutes." I had the opportunity to respond to her, and I said, "There are absolutes. One absolute is the law of gravity, and it has been proven. No one here today would challenge or defy the law of gravity by jumping off the many-storied building next door. If one did jump, we would agree that whether he or she believed it or not, death absolutely would be the result, every time." I just could not keep silent and let her statement go unchallenged. Ignorance is not bliss, and what you don't know can hurt you.

I am not the only one who believes in absolutes. Ravi Zacharias, India-born Canadian-American, author, and Christian apologist, spoke at the University of Louisville [Kentucky] some years ago. He talked about absolutes and focused on the four he held to be the most important: (1) evil, (2) justice, (3) love, and (4) forgiveness.[33]

A Leap to Faith

Soren Kierkegaard, a 19th Century Danish philosopher, theologian, and poet wrote about faith. He is attributed with coining the phrase, "A leap of faith." Kierkegaard never used that exact phrase, but he did use the phrase: "A leap to faith," meaning moving from an absence of faith to faith or belief.[34] No matter how you phrase it, it takes a leap of faith to get above the rubble and on to higher ground. And it takes an even greater leap of faith to imagine dancing on the rubble even before it happens.

Self-centeredness, or narcissism, can be our greatest enemy. The Bible warns us not to rely on self. "Trust in the Lord with all your heart and lean not on your own understanding. In all your ways acknowledge Him and He shall direct your paths." (Proverbs 3: 5-6). The Hebrew word for direct means God will straighten out your path. When we rely on God, we receive what He can do, but when we rely on self, we receive only what self can do.

God will absolutely help us when we listen to Him. I am regretful for anyone who doesn't listen to God and who depends on self because self is limited, God's power is not. I woke up this morning saying the word "ubiquitous." It is not a word I often use, and I wasn't sure of the exact meaning, so I looked up synonyms for the word. Some of them are as follows: omnipresent, universal, pervasive, global, abundant, permeating, and ever-present. God is absolutely all of this and much more. I took my time and used each synonym in prayer and thanked God for being all that He is to me. You might want to use this plan for your next devotion. You will be surprised how it will bless you. If your image of God is small when you start, it won't be small when you finish. There are absolutes, and Henri Frederic Amiel (1821-1881) Swiss Philosopher, poet, and critic said it best: "There is no repose for the mind except in the absolute, for feelings, except in the infinite, for the soul, except in the divine." The universe is made up of absolutes, and so is life itself. Without absolutes there would be chaos. Without absolutes there could be no God.

God is an absolute for every believer, and the Apostle Paul put it like this: "If in this life only we have hope in Christ, we are of all men most pitiable. But now Christ is risen from the dead and has become the first-fruits of those who have fallen asleep [died]." (I Corinthians 15:19,20) No God, no "repose for the mind," said Paul to the Corinthians. I can't imagine what it would be like not to believe in a God who loves and cares for us. I would be absolutely miserable. Not believing that there is a God who loves and cares for us is a hopeless way to live. Perpetual worry would result. Science and the medical professions have noted that over one hundred diseases have been directly attributed to worry.

Worry comes when we fail to listen and absolutely trust in God. A lack of trust brings about doubt and hopelessness. We must believe that He is real, and that He rewards those who diligently seek Him. (Hebrews 11:6) An elderly lady I once knew said, "I always feel bad when I feel good, for I know that I'll feel bad after a while." That's no way to live! The bottom line is this: when you worry, either you don't believe there is a God, or you don't believe His Word. Worry erodes the soul and brings on depression, discouragement, despondency, and even suicide. Worry is a destructive emotion that you do not want to nurture.

> Worry implies that we don't quite trust God is big enough, powerful enough, or loving enough to take care of what's happening in our lives. Francis Chan

Personal Application: Prayerfully write down your answers to the following questions.

1. In your own words, what do you think was going through David's mind when he heard Goliath cursing God and Israel?

2. What do you think enabled David at such a young age to have the confidence in God to face Goliath? Do you think David was worried about the outcome?

3. Do you think that many of David's Psalms were words he heard while listening to God?

4. In your personal life, have you experienced a time when you desperately needed God and He responded to that need? In what way(s) did He respond?

Read Ahead (small group): Read Chapter 5: Keep Learning
The space below is provided to write any thoughts or insights that you might have from reading Chapter 5.

_____

_____

_____

Take this Survey:
Ranking yourself from 1 to 10: how satisfied are you with "listening?"

1 being "I seldom listen" and 10 being "I always listen." Circle one number.

1   2   3   4   5   6   7   8   9   10

Comments _____

_____

Essential references: Proverbs 1:5; James 1:9; Matthew 11:15; Proverbs 1:8-9; John 8:47; Proverbs 19:20

Chapter 5

Keep Learning

> Unlettered doesn't mean unlearned!

It is possible to be educated with academic degrees running out of your proverbial ears and not be learned. Multiple degrees in religion do not make you a theologian either. And having no formal education somehow elevates you to the level of king Solomon's court as one of his wise men. Actually, we are learning throughout our lives, either by osmosis or we are learning through books.

The key to learning begins with an open mind. We can't study and not learn something. Learning will force us to go outside of our known boundaries to the unknown and search for truth. If you are a truth seeker, you will know the truth and the truth will make you free. (John 8:31-32) It's essential that we examine our views or beliefs often to determine whether our beliefs line up with Scripture [truth]. We should practice this throughout life.

We may encounter any or all three of the major hindrances Satan puts in front of us. They are: deception, temptation, and accusation. We can choose not to allow these hindrances to affect us because we have God-given authority over all three. "Behold, I give you the authority to trample on serpents and scorpions, and over all the power of the enemy and nothing shall by any means hurt you." (Luke 10:19)

The best way to test our understanding of truth is to personally compare our behavior with that of Jesus, who is the Truth, not by what we read, what family has told us, or what a person whom we admire has told us. Life is a school of endless "tests and exams." The purpose of life-long tests is to help us to know what is important to keep and what isn't. We can't trust the mind to tell us the truth. Our minds react to what is in them. When we think about what we believe, we have a responsibility to ourselves to determine the veracity of those beliefs because we tend to indiscriminately accept what we have learned (hoarded). A lie can be just as pleasing and just as addictive as the truth because our minds can accept a lie as being the truth.

The hoarding of "feel good" religious rules impedes and obstructs our usefulness to God. Just as we hoard material stuff in life, we hoard religious stuff, too. Therefore, since we occasionally purge the material stuff that we accumulate in life, we also must get rid of stuff in our spiritual lives that are not true and, therefore, useless. It's amazing how many "feel good" whatnots and souvenirs we save over the years. We hold on to things that we don't have room for anymore. They are precious to us, but other things must take their place, things that we need. So, the decision has to be made to turn loose of the things we don't use and will never need.

It's the same with the "feel good" religious rules that we were taught, rules that wouldn't send us to hell yet are not good enough to send us to heaven. Like material memories that bring us pleasure, religious rules do the same. When we began our journey with Christ, the rules seemed o.k., but then one day we were enlightened by the Holy Spirit that certain rules we were living by were not necessary and could even be detrimental to our spiritual journeys. Hoarding, whether material or religious, can be harmful at times. The acid test of truth is an experience with truth personified, Jesus Christ. You will know the truth (Jesus), and He will set you free. Only Jesus can show us the truth. Period! He is not just someone in whom we believe; He is someone whom we experience.

It is amazing how much stuff Kaye and I have accumulated over the fifty-eight years we've been married. Things that we thought we could not do without at the time are now stored in our basement, garage, or stuffed in a closet. Not too long ago we decided it was time to "downsize." So, we went to work sorting and getting rid of those things that we were not using anymore. It is the same process we go through when we check our spiritual lives. We discover rules that we have stored in our memory that felt good at the time and are rules that we planned to keep forever. They are rules that we have cherished and thought would save us, but they could not, so now they must go. The decision to turn loose of either one, the material and/or religious is painful, but doing both may be needed if they are a hinderance to us. Hopefully, we have learned that letting go is not a bad thing at all, but instead it is a blessing. This "letting go" process is called spiritual growth. Paul talks about the importance of spiritual growth. He said when he became a man "He put away childish things." (I Corinthians 13:11) Sometimes we just have to decide to grow up and that requires trashing our playthings.

God has a voice, and it is a deep-seated impression that teaches us the direction in which to go. We must learn to listen to that voice and obey it. God has a voice and one way in which we can hear God speak is to open our Bibles, because when we open them, the Author will show up and He will speak to us. I've heard it said that what you don't know won't hurt you. Wrong! Ignorance is not bliss

> "The greatest problem today is Bible literacy."
> Elmer Towns

When we trust the Lord, we will never lose because we will always either win the battle, or we will learn an important lesson during the process. Sometimes that learning process is spiritually painful. The Apostle Paul learned a lot through suffering. He spoke of his past, but he spent most of his time talking about the future. He wrote to the Philippians from jail, "Brethren, I count not myself to have apprehended: but this one thing I do, forgetting those things which are behind, and reaching forth unto those things which are before." (Philippians 3:13) Man-made religion has a way of making learning sterile. Knowledge is fluid and when we limit it, it becomes stagnant and learning stops. To compensate for the lack of the truth, the lie prevails, and all sorts of opinions gather around what is left of the truth. And the truth that remains is often distorted and spiritually destructive. What was once pure and clearly understood as God's Word, now becomes unrecognizable.

Paul saw that happen in his day, and we see it happening in ours. So, that is why it is important to check to see if we are still "in the faith." We can be deceived and not know it. We can believe a lie and teach it. We can devote our lives to a lie and feel righteous about it. I did for several years before I allowed myself to face the truth that good deeds couldn't save me.

Truth sets us free; religion can shackle us to man-made rules. If we think we could never be deceived, we are deceived already. My greatest fear is to be in a church where the presence of God used to be.

> A lie can feel as good as the truth when we are deceived.

It is critically important to study and learn [and unlearn] all you can. Your eternity depends on it. That is why Paul admonished Timothy to "Be diligent to present yourself approved to God, a worker who does not need to be ashamed, rightly dividing the word of truth." (II Timothy 2:14) Benjamin Franklin, who we know had a way with words, put it this way: "Tell me and I will forget; teach me and I will remember; involve me, and I will learn."

Visualize a runner in the Olympics nearing the finish line reaching forward, straining every muscle as he races to cross the finish line first to win the prize. That is what Paul is saying. He admonishes the Philippians to keep their eyes on the prize in front of them, not on the past. Sadly, some people are "always learning and never able to come to the knowledge of the truth." (II Timothy 3:7)

When we read the first part of Philippians Chapter 3, Paul refers briefly to his past [he looks in the rear-view mirror]. He says, "Circumcised the eighth day, of the stock of Israel, of the tribe of Benjamin, a Hebrew of the Hebrews; concerning the law, a Pharisee. Concerning zeal, persecuting the church, concerning the righteousness which is in the law, blameless." (vv.5-6)

The next word is very important. He says, "BUT [he spent the majority of his writings looking out of the windshield into the future] what things were gain to me, these I have counted loss for Christ. Yet indeed I also count all things loss for the excellence of the knowledge of Christ Jesus my Lord, for whom I have suffered the loss of all things, and count them as dung [rubbish], that I may gain Christ." (3:5-8) Paul learned to dance on the rubble. The price we pay to learn can be painful, but not to learn can be even more painful.

"Who Is Malala?"

"Who is Malala?" the masked Taliban assassin shouted. The gunman had jumped on Malala's school bus and shouted her name. The bus was loaded with Pakistani girls headed for home. The gunman's sole purpose was to assassinate a fifteen-year-old girl who was defiantly opposing the

Taliban's ban on education for girls.

Malala was easy to spot because she was the only girl on the bus whose face was uncovered. She intentionally had not worn her head scarf since beginning her protest. Malala had been very vocal against the ban on education for Pakistani girls. She had bravely spoken out against this injustice on local media. Therefore, she was well known in the community for her passion for education. However, to openly defy the Taliban leaders was a death sentence.

Upon identifying Malala, the gunman pointed his gun at her and fired three shots point blank. Miraculously, she survived a bullet to the head. It happened on October 9, 2012. She was sent to Queen Elizabeth Hospital in the United Kingdom where she made an amazing recovery. The bullet of the Taliban assassin did not stop Malala. She continues her crusade for equal education opportunity for all girls worldwide. On July 12, 2013, Malala spoke at the United Nations to call for worldwide access to education. Her comment regarding her ordeal was this: "God did not want me dead."[35] Malala is dancing on the rubble of an assassin's attempt on her life.

Merle Shain, author of *When Lovers Are Friends*, phrased it this way: "There are only two ways to approach life—as a victim or as a gallant fighter—and you must decide if you want to act or react . . . a lot of people forget that."[36] I find when I hurt, I write! I never really understood compassion or pain until I experienced pain for myself. There is a Scripture that refers to Jesus that surprised me, but at the same time encouraged me, and that is Hebrews 5:8 where the writer says, "Although He was a Son, yet He learned obedience by the things which he suffered."

Paul Claudel, a Roman Catholic French poet, author, and dramatist explained the suffering of Jesus this way: "Jesus did not come to explain away suffering or remove it. He came to fulfill it with His presence. Pain can be a transforming agent if we will let it teach us."[37] Pain has a voice. It is impossible to tell others that we know how they feel if we haven't suffered their loss or pain. Life does have its limits. Pain can expand our horizons by transforming us into the image of Jesus. We learn obedience like He did through suffering. We are imperfect beings and we are limited, but God is not limited. That is why we must draw our strength from Him. If Jesus went through sufferings, and learned from them, why should we expect anything less?

The reason why life is so frustrating at times is because we can't equate the life of Jesus with our own life. We think Jesus had a life without a struggle, at least until He was crucified. But Jesus fought the Adversary all the way until His last breath and His last words: "It is finished." We think that Jesus was never tempted the way we are, but the Bible says: "For we do not have a High Priest who cannot sympathize with our weaknesses, but was in all points tempted as we are, yet without sin." (Hebrews 4:15)

Think about it: "For by grace we are saved through faith. Therefore, we have peace with God through our Lord Jesus Christ . . . and not only that, but we also glory in tribulations, knowing that tribulations produce perseverance; and perseverance, character; and character hope." (Romans 5:1, 3-4)

As a side note, I'm not a professional writer, but I write. I say this for the sake of those who think it takes a pro to write. Anyone can write notes in a journal. You would be surprised how valuable those notes will be and bless you later in life, even inspire you to write books, magazine articles, or material for a blog or a book. Some of my favorite gems are found in my old Bibles where I scribbled thoughts. They are fresh inspiration even though some of them were written a half-century ago.

For example, just today I went down into our basement where we have everything imaginable stored, and I noticed a large flip chart with the following written on it in bold letters:

You can count on three things that will never change:

1. God loves you.
2. God is in control.
3. God is all you will ever need.

We can learn from everybody and everything. Learning is amazing and unlimited! I learned the following on the Internet from Jeff Goins, who is a writer himself:

- Part of writing is not writing.
- All good writing is rewriting.
- Write until it looks complete.

There has never been a greater opportunity to gather knowledge with all the technology that is available today, and it's essentially free. Many a life is ruined because of being satisfied with little things. I have a sign that I have carried with me for years that I always display where I can see it. The sign has two simple words: THINK BIG!

There seems to be a level of learning that we can only experience through suffering. Somehow, when we trust God with our pain there comes a joy and strength that we would not know otherwise. There is a peace that passes all understanding within the pain that can't be explained except by knowing Christ. So dear one, God knows you hurt, He feels your pain. His grace is sufficient. God will work your pain together with all other aspects of your life that will be for your good and ultimately to His glory. Just keep on learning and dancing on the rubble.

One of the first life Scriptures that I memorized as a young Christian was I Corinthians 10:13: "No temptation has overtaken you except such as is common to man; but God is faithful, who will not allow you to be tempted beyond what you are able but will with the temptation also make the way of escape, that you may be able to bear it." The prophet Isaiah writes: "But those who wait on the Lord shall renew their strength; they shall mount up with wings like eagles, they shall run and not be weary, they shall walk and not faint." (Isaiah 40:31)

The Fire That Won't Go Out
Like Moses' burning bush that wouldn't go out, there was an unquenchable fire for learning ignited in my soul the day that Dad burned my schoolbooks. It happened in the fall before my senior year of high school. That summer things were bad at our house. My mother was forced to leave home and take my baby brother with her to stay with her mother for a few weeks until Dad settled down from his alcohol binge. This left five of us children at home with Dad. There were four girls and me.

One day, while he was drunk, Dad was playing with his 12-gauge shotgun and it accidentally went off with the buckshot barely missing us. He had shot a huge hole in the kitchen screen door. It scared him so bad that he told my sister Kate to hide the shotgun shells from him. She did. The next day when everyone was in school, except me, he decided that he wanted the shells, and he asked me for them. I tried to explain to him that I didn't know where they were, but he went into a rage and picked up my .22 rifle and smashed it. After he destroyed my rifle, he began to curse me and threatened to whip me. The Bible says for the parents not to provoke their children to wrath, but that is what happened in this case.

I left home and my best friend James invited me to stay with him. His mother, Lola Pennington, was very understanding and asked me what I was going to do. I told her that I wanted to go to my grandmother's house where my mother and baby brother were staying. The next morning, Mrs. Pennington packed me a lunch and gave me a toothbrush and two dollars. She took me to the West Virginia and Kentucky state line and let me out there so I could hitchhike the rest of the way. I caught a ride on a coal truck on top of Bradshaw Mountain, and the driver took me most of the way. I walked the last few miles to Grandma Potter's house.

When I arrived, Mother was shocked to see me. I told her what had happened and that I could not return home. She was heartbroken at what had happened and immediately returned home to make sure the other children were all right. My grandparents agreed to keep me the rest of the summer and let me enroll in high school there. That fall, Mother wrote asking me to come home. I wrote back explaining that I could not return unless Dad agreed to it. One day a letter came from her saying that she had bought some used high school books for me and that Dad said it was all right for me to return to go to school. I was thrilled.

My Uncle Scooter took me back to West Virginia so I could enroll in school. When I arrived, Dad was drunk, as he was when I had left, and he brought up the incident that caused me to leave home. He instructed my mother to go and get the books she had bought. She brought them to me, and Dad asked me to put them in the yard near the big rock on which he had broken my rifle. I obeyed him and he gathered up some paper and set fire to the books. I watched them burn! I knew I couldn't stay there and go to school. Uncle Scooter told me that it would be better if I went back to Grandmother's house with him. I did.

I was angry with my father for burning my schoolbooks that day, but something good came out of it. My father didn't know it, but he ignited two fires that day. One fire burned my books and went out shortly afterward. The other fire ignited an unquenchable thirst for learning that continues to burn bright and hot within me to this day. What I am about to share now is to give honor to God for His faithfulness. Dad and I reconciled after the burning books incident. He lost his job in the coal mine in West Virginia, and the family had to move back to Kentucky where I was living with my grandmother. I finished my senior year at home with my family.

Ever since the day that Dad burned my books, I have realized their value and the value of a good education. The fire of learning is still burning within even as I envision the smoldering textbooks in the recesses of my memory. To God is the glory!

Learning Isn't Optional

Some Christians believe that formal learning is not a spiritual endeavor. Their philosophy is, "Open your mouth and the Lord will fill it." In other words, we don't need to study, all we have to do is open our mouths and God will fill it with words the moment we preach, teach, or witness about Christ. That is like saying a football player does not have to wear a helmet. He wears everything else that a football player wears, but no helmet. In a real game he would not last very long. When we hear someone speak who holds the view that learning isn't necessary, we realize that he (or she) didn't wear a helmet during the "game." It takes study and hard work to win in the game of life.

What has been amazing to me for over more than fifty years of ministry is how some of the greatest art, literature, inventions, and medical marvels have come about through people who have suffered unbelievable pain. They learned to turn their sufferings and setbacks around to be a blessing in their lives and the lives of others. If we refuse to become bitter when something bad happens to us, and we trust God through it all, something marvelous will arise from our pain and hurt. Jesus promises us that it will. The hardest thing in life is to learn which bridge to cross and which bridge to burn. Life is tough, my friend, but so are we all with God's help.

> There are two little words that make the biggest mountains disappear and they are: "try" and "trust."

Study Guide: Keep Learning

Key Quote(s): "Be diligent to present yourself approved to God, a worker who does not need to be ashamed, rightly dividing the word of truth." 2 Timothy 2:15

Begin with Prayer
O, Lord, blessed and wise God teach me to know and learn Your ways. Help me to guard my mouth lest I sin with my tongue and bring reproach on Your name. Teach me Your wisdom and ways, O Lord, and I will walk in Your truth. You, O wise Father, know all things and I want to learn from You. As the deer pants for the water brooks, my heart cries out to You for wisdom and understanding of Your word. My heart overflows with joy when I remember the greatness of your strength. I want to clap my hands, dance, and shout with a voice of triumph when I behold the vastness of Your creation and mercy to me. Open Your Word to me, guide me with Your wisdom and counsel, and help me to keep on learning. In the name of Jesus. Amen.

Author: Unknown. Most likely the prophet Jonah or a prophetic associate of his.

Date: About 760 BC or after 612 BC

Inspiration: Jonah 1:1-12; 15-17
¹ Now the word of the Lord came to Jonah the son of Amittai, saying,
² "Arise, go to Nineveh, that great city and cry out against it; for their wickedness has come up before me."
³ But Jonah arose to flee to Tarshish from the presence of the Lord. He went down to Joppa, and found a ship going to Tarshish; so he paid the fare, and went down into it, to go with them to Tarshish from the presence of the Lord.
⁴ But the Lord sent out a great wind on the sea, and there was a mighty tempest on the sea, so that the ship was about to be broken up.
⁵ Then the mariners were afraid; and every man cried out to his god and threw the cargo that was in the ship into the sea, to lighten the load. But Jonah had gone down into the lowest parts of the ship, had lain down,

and was fast asleep.

6 So the captain came to him, and said to him, "What do you mean, sleeper? Arise, call on your God, perhaps your God will consider us, so that we may not perish."

7 And they said to one another, "Come, let us cast lots, that we may know for whose cause this trouble has come upon us." So, they cast lots, and the lot fell on Jonah.

8 Then they said to him, "Please tell us! For whose cause is this trouble upon us? What is your occupation? And where do you come from? What is your country? And of what people are you?"

9 So he said to them, "I am a Hebrew; and I fear the Lord, the God of heaven, who made the sea and the dry land."

10 Then the men were exceedingly afraid, and said to him, "Why have you done this?" For the men knew that he fled from the presence of the Lord, because he had told them.

11 Then they said to him, "What shall we do to you that the sea may be calm for us?" –for the sea was growing more tempestuous.

12 And he said to them, "Pick me up and throw me into the sea; then the sea will become calm for you. For I know that this great tempest is because of me."

15 So they picked up Jonah and threw him into the sea, and the sea ceased from its raging.

16 Then the men feared the Lord exceedingly and offered a sacrifice to the Lord and took vows.

17 Now the Lord had prepared a great fish to swallow Jonah. And Jonah was in the belly of the fish three days and three nights.

Jonah 2: 1, 10
1 Then Jonah prayed to the Lord his God from the fish's belly.
10 So the Lord spoke to the fish and it vomited Jonah onto dry land.

Jonah 3: 1-5; 10
1 Now the word of the Lord came to Jonah the second time saying,
2 "Arise, go to Nineveh, that great city, and preach to it the message that I tell you."
3 So Jonah arose and went to Nineveh, according to the word of the Lord. Now Nineveh was an exceedingly great city, a three-day journey *in extent.*

[4] And Jonah began to enter the city on the first day's walk. Then he cried out and said, "Yet forty days and Nineveh shall be overthrown."
[5] So the people of Nineveh believed God, proclaimed a fast, and put on sackcloth, from the greatest to the least of them.
[10] Then God saw their [the Ninevites] works, that they turned from their evil way, and God relented from the disaster that he had said He would bring upon them, and He did not do it.

Jonah 4:1-11

[1] But it displeased Jonah exceedingly, and he became angry.
[2] So he prayed to the Lord, and said, "Ah, Lord, was not this what I said when I was still in my country? Therefore, I fled previously to Tarshish, for I knew that You are a gracious and merciful God, slow to anger and abundant loving-kindness. One who relents from doing harm.
[3] "Therefore now, O Lord, please take my life from me, for it is better for me to die than to live."
[4] Then the Lord said, "Is it right for you to be angry?"
[5] So Jonah went out of the city and sat on the east side of the city. There he made himself a shelter and sat under it in the shade, till he might see what would become of the city.
[6] And the Lord God prepared a plant and made it come up over Jonah, that it might be shade for his head to deliver him from his misery. So Jonah was very grateful for the plant.
[7] But as morning dawned the next day God prepared a worm, and it so damaged the plant that it withered.
[8] And it happened, when the sun arose, that God prepared a vehement east wind; and the sun beat on Jonah's head, so that he grew faint. Then he wished death for himself, and said, "It is better for me to die than to live."
[9] Then God said to Jonah, "Is it right for you to be angry about the plant?" And he [Jonah] said, "It is right for me to be angry, even to death."
[10] But the Lord said, "You have had pity on the plant for which you have not labored, nor made it grow, which came up in a night and perished in a night.
[11] "And should I not pity Nineveh, that great city, in which are more than one hundred and twenty thousand persons who cannot discern between their right hand and their left—and much livestock?"

Backstory:
There are many ways to gain knowledge and among them are the following three ways:

> ➤ Learning
> ➤ Unlearning
> ➤ Relearning

Our brains are always analyzing and processing information and images. We can never think about nothing. We are ever learning, unlearning, and relearning. We see these three ways embodied in Jonah's life.

Keep in Mind
- In Hebrew, Jonah's name means "dove."
- Jonah was a prophet of the Northern Kingdom of Israel.
- Nineveh was a Gentile city; Jonah was the only prophet sent by God to preach to the Gentiles.
- Assyria [Nineveh] was a constant threat to Israel; Jonah hated the Ninevites.
- Jonah learned, unlearned, and relearned painfully in both body and spirit.

Learning
Jonah's classroom: the great fish that swallowed him.

God called Jonah to take a short but direct message from God to the people of Nineveh: "Yet forty days, and Nineveh shall be overthrown." (3:5) Jonah didn't want to take this message to them because Assyria was Israel's mortal enemy, and he knew that if the Ninevites repented of their evil acts, God would have mercy on them and spare them. Jonah decided that he would rather run from God than do as He asked when he boarded a ship to Tarshish, a city in a completely different direction from Nineveh. He did so because his sole purpose was to escape the will of God.

The Scripture states that "a great storm came, and the people feared for their lives." (1:6) It didn't take Jonah long to admit that he was the cause of the storm because he was fleeing from God's calling. To save the ship from the storm, Jonah suggested that the men of the ship throw him overboard. (2:5) The crew obliged Jonah and threw him over the side. The storm ceased. It is likely that Jonah was fully prepared to die by drowning, but God had "prepared a great fish to swallow him. And Jonah was in the belly of the fish three days and three nights." (1:17)

We might say that God prepared a three-day intensive seminar for Jonah in the belly of the fish with new learning skills and a new and improved attitude toward God. Jonah's contemporaries, Hosea and Amos, had predicted that Assyria would punish Israel for their disobedience. Jonah was fully aware that his country, Israel, would suffer at the hand of the Assyrians. Hating the Assyrians as he did, and knowing that God was a merciful God, Jonah didn't want the Assyrians to escape the God-promised punishment if they repented. If he didn't deliver God's message to the Ninevites, then they wouldn't have a reason to repent, and the Ninevites would be punished.

And, so, Jonah found himself in the fish's belly, praying and beseeching God. It may be hard to believe that a man could survive inside of a great fish for three days and three nights. There are those who have concerns about a human being swallowed by a "great fish" despite the New Testament suggesting it was a whale. (Matthew 12:40) A whale is a mammal, not a fish. But there is written record of a seaman, in 1891, who was swallowed by a large sperm whale near the Falkland Islands. After three days he was found, unconscious but alive, though there was damage to his skin.[35] Ill-conceived arguments lie in the fact that both the Hebrew word *dag* and the Greek word *ketos* are generic terms that can apply to any aquatic creature. Some, however, dispute the credibility of both stories.

Unlearning
Jonah's teacher: a merciful God

Jonah finally learned his lesson that running from God and one's calling wasn't smart. Scriptures back that fact up: "for the gifts and calling of God are irrevocable." (Romans 11:29) Jonah positioned himself on a hilltop overlooking Nineveh where he could watch the fire of God's judgment fall out of heaven on them. His education had gone from elementary to advanced learning. He learned not to run from God; he was about to learn that God was merciful beyond his imagination.

As Jonah sat in the blazing sun watching Nineveh from above waiting for the city's destruction, God caused a shady plant to grow up and give him some relief from the sun. The next day, God called on a worm to cut it down. Jonah was upset by this and began to complain. Then God rebuked Jonah for his complaining and pointed out to him that he was more concerned about the worm and the vine than he was about the thousands of people. God could have reminded Jonah about what He said in Deuteronomy 28:47: "Because you did not serve the Lord your God with gladness of heart, for the abundance of everything, therefore you shall serve your enemies, whom the Lord will send against you. . . ."

Relearning
Our teacher: Jehovah, a merciful God to all nations

Some of the lessons we learn in life are timeless, such as "For God so loved the world He gave His only begotten Son, that whoever believes in Him should not perish but have eternal life." (John 3:16) Another timeless lesson is God's promise to Abraham that in him [Abraham] "all the families of the earth would be blessed." (Genesis 12:3b) Then there are time-lessons that are lessons that we have relearned, and they can only be learned over a period of time. Jonah experienced this principle as he sat on the hill overlooking Nineveh wishing he were dead when God reminded him that people were more important than a plant or worm. People do change.

The book of Jonah is filled with timeless lessons. Jonah did not want to spare the Ninevites because they were Israel's worst enemy and, after all, they were Gentiles. But when Jonah relented, it released the Holy Spirit and the people of Nineveh were convicted of their evil ways. They repented and the city was spared.

What can be frightening is to be responsible for holding back people from knowing God's mercy because we were unwilling to relent and forgive our enemies. Jonah experienced God's mercy on a people who did not believe in his God. How many times have we felt and acted as Jonah, wishing God would pronounce judgment on our enemies? Then we grow in knowledge, and over time we realize how merciful and forgiving God is to us. We relearn that the grace we once knew is not just grace for us but is really "great grace" (Acts 4:33b) that is available for even our worst enemies. See poem, "Great Grace" in the section **Poems**

From and For the Heart.)

Consider this. The three ways we learn can be compared to fishing. Suppose we go fishing with a net [learning] and cast out the net and bring in the catch [knowledge]. Then we sort the contents [knowledge, unlearning] and we take the best of what we caught home with us. Some of what is in the net is digestible, but not all. Over time we learn a better way to fish [relearning]. We don't completely throw away our fishing business; instead, we make the necessary changes [knowledge, relearning] that results in a better fishing method.

Jesus validated the story of Jonah when he referenced Jonah in Matthew 12:39-41. Jesus said, "For as Jonah was three days and three nights in the belly of the great fish, so will the Son of Man be three days in the heart of the earth." Jesus hints that the three days Jonah spent in the fish's belly was a sign to Nineveh. Jesus said, "for as Jonah became a sign to the Ninevites, so also the Son of Man will be to this generation." (Luke 11:30) Somehow, the Ninevites heard about Jonah's experience that caused them to take him seriously and repent. As Jonah was a sign to Nineveh, Jesus's resurrection is a sign for us today.

Personal Application: Prayerfully write down your answers to the following questions,

1. In this season of your life, what is the greatest learning obstacle you are facing internally and/or externally?

2. Give an example in your own life in which adversity taught you how to feel the pain of others.

3. What is one thing that you feel God wants you to unlearn and why?

4. What is one thing that you have relearned that has improved your relationship with Jesus?

Read Ahead (small group): Read Chapter 6: Keep Leaning

The space below is provided to write any thoughts or insights you receive from reading Chapter 6.

_____

_____

_____

Take this Survey

Ranking yourself from 1 to 10, how satisfied are you with the way you are living your life right now? 1 being "I am very dissatisfied" and 10 being "I'm very satisfied." Circle one number.

1   2   3   4   5   6   7   8   9   10

Comments _____

_____

Essential References: Philippians 4:9; Psalm 32:8; Proverbs 1:7; Psalm 25:5; Colossians 3:16; Psalm 143:10; Jonah 14:26; Proverbs 12:1

Chapter 6

Keep Leaning

Even Birds Lean on God

The following story begins with lumberjacks in the forest cutting down trees. They came across a tree which had a bird nest with several eggs in it. One of the men proceeded to cut down the tree anyway, but another man stepped in and asked that the tree be spared until the eggs hatched. He explained that they could come back later and cut it down, and so, the eggs were spared.

Several days later the crew came back to harvest the lone tree that they had left to give time for the eggs to hatch. And hatched they did. But there was a surprise awaiting the burly lumberjacks. Inside the nest in plain sight was a little white piece of paper woven into the bird nest. It was a piece of a Sunday school leaflet and on it was this phrase: "We put our trust in God." Praise the Lord!

Jesus said, "Look at the birds of the air, for they neither sow nor reap nor gather into barns; yet your heavenly Father feeds them. Are you not of more value than they?" (Matthew 6:26) What can be learned from this story?

_____

_____

_____

> Worry is probably the number one reason
> why we find it so difficult to lean on God.

The Bible doesn't down-play problems; instead, it shows us how to deal with them. The Scriptures say, "These things I have spoken to you, that in Me you may have peace. In the world you will have tribulation;

but be of good cheer, I have overcome the world." (John 16:33) Trials and tribulations are real, and we fight them every day of our lives, but the Bible admonishes us not to worry about the troubles and trials that we face. The main emphasis is on the last part of that verse, "Be of good cheer, I have overcome the world." Jesus is saying don't worry; I've got you covered. Jesus is standing already victorious. Therefore, we can joy in that victory because we are heirs and joint heirs with Christ. (Romans 8:17). According to this verse we share in the suffering of Christ now and will share in the glory later when we join Him in heaven.

Worry comes from an old English word that means to struggle. Wolves kill sheep by biting them around the neck and holding on until the sheep die. That is what worry does; it grabs us by the spiritual throat and strangles the very life out of us. The first thing that we notice is our joy is gone. The Bible says that the joy of the Lord is our strength. No joy, no strength, no life. Life is about choices, not just will-power. We choose, and God gives us the ability to do what we are willing to try.

> Worry makes a small thing cast a big shadow.

Worry Is Contagious
All one needs to do is put on a worried face and, before we know it, other faces will take on the same look. I observed recently how worried parents can affect their children. I saw the difference between one of the mothers who was very positive; her children were also positive. The other mother worried about everything and her children worried also. It's the same with fathers. A positive attitude is also contagious.

Recently I was watching the reality show *Shark Tank* on ABC TV. It is a program with five entrepreneurs of industry who make dreams a reality for budding entrepreneurs who come to the "shark tank" to get financial support to make their dreams come true. Last week I watched three young siblings pitch an invention their father had created called Cup Board Pro. The father, Kevin Young, a retired fireman who passed away from cancer related to the 9-11 Twin Tower tragedy, had died three months earlier. Sadly, the children had lost their mother to breast cancer in 2012.

The father's dream was to appear on *Shark Tank* and present his invention, but he died before he had the chance. So, his three children, Kaley, Christian, and Keira came in his place to present their father's idea. By the time the three told their story, there was not a dry eye on the Shark panel. And within forty-eight hours, Cup Board Pro recorded over a million dollars in sales. Even Amazon sold out. The Sharks, all five of them, came together and invested $100,000.00 for 20% in the company with the 20% to be donated to firefighter charities. How we view life does influence others.

The way to deal with worry is to put it into God's loving hands. Elizabeth Elliot was a Christian author and speaker. Jim Elliot was killed in 1956 while attempting to contact the Auca Indians of eastern Ecuador. Elizabeth later spent two years as a missionary to the tribe who killed her husband. She died at the age of eighty-eight. She said, "Put your concerns in the hands that were wounded for you." Wonderful advice, but not always easy to do.

> The God to whom children say their prayers
> has a face similar to their mothers'.

Victory with Jesus

The Amazon River is the largest river in the entire world. The mouth of the river is 90 miles across. There is enough water to exceed the combined flow of the Yangtze, Mississippi, and the Nile Rivers. So much water comes from the Amazon that they can detect its currents 200 miles out in the Atlantic Ocean.

One irony of ancient navigation is that sailors in those times died for lack of water. The reason: the ships were caught in windless waters of the South Atlantic. Therefore, they were adrift, helpless, and dying of thirst. Sometimes other ships from South America who knew the area would come alongside and call out, "What's your problem?" They would answer back, "Can you spare us some water? We are dying of thirst." And from the other ship came the cry, "Just lower your buckets! You are at the mouth of the mighty Amazon River."

Jesus is the fountain of living water; He is present right now to supply our need if we will only lower our faith bucket for Him to fill. For example, Jesus told the woman at the well that He could give her living water so that she would never thirst again. (John 4:10) The key: She had to ask for it. In His Sermon on the Mount Jesus said, "Ask and it will be given you. . . ." (Matthew 7:7a)

Living Water

Israel knows something about leaning on God. Peter Colon wrote a beautiful article in *Israel My Glory* (September/ October 2015), entitled: "*Sukkah Shalom.*" It is an Invitation In which he explains that Sukkot (Feast of Tabernacles) has three main elements: booths, water, and light.

He says that "the most joyous season in ancient Israel was that of the Feast of Tabernacles. It fell during the time of year when hearts were naturally full of thanksgiving, joy, and expectation." This is what he says about the element of water. He explains that the ancient rabbis believed that "he who has not seen the rejoicing at the place of the water-drawing has never seen rejoicing in his life."

In Jesus' day, the Feast of Tabernacles included an elaborate water ritual. Each morning at the festival a priest emerged from the Water Gate on the south side of the Temple carrying a gold pitcher. He led a joyous procession to the Pool of Siloam in the Old City of David. Then he descended to the pool and drew water into the pitcher while everyone charged toward the pool. "Therefore, with joy you will draw water from the wells of salvation" (Isaiah 12:3).

When the priest returned to the Temple around the time of the morning sacrifice, someone blew the shofar [ram's horn]. Then another priest, carrying the drink offering of wine, joined him. Together they ascended the ramp of the Great Altar and poured their libations into funnels.

The mixture of liquids flowed down to the Kidron Valley. Several other priests, holding willow branches, marched once around the altar reciting, "Save now [*Hashanah*], I pray, O LORD, O LORD, I pray, send now prosperity" (Psalms 118:25). As the Levites played their musical instruments, the people sang the *Hallel*: Psalms 113 through 118. The water ritual was emblematic of the Holy Spirit. Israel's leaders believed God would pour out the Holy Spirit on Israel and the nations during the Messianic Kingdom.

"In that day," when the Messiah comes with all His saints and His feet stand on the Mount of Olives (Zechariah 14:4), luminaries will dim (vv.6-7) and "living waters shall flow from Jerusalem" (v. 8).

One year, on the final and climactic day of Sukkot, as the Jewish people were expecting the outpouring of God's Spirit, Jesus stood up and shouted, "if anyone thirst, let him come to Me and drink." (John 7:37) The invitation still stands today so that whosoever comes to Jesus may freely drink of the water of eternal life.

Leaning Leads to Transforming

When we drink from the fountain of living water it is the first step toward change that takes us from glory to glory. Paul describes the move from glory to glory using the word "transformed," or "changed." It is the Greek word *metamorphoo*. Paul writes, "But we all, with unveiled face beholding as in a mirror the glory of the Lord, are being transformed into the same image from glory to glory, just as by the Spirit of the Lord." To better understand what the Apostle Paul is teaching the Corinthians, we will look at two words and their Greek meaning. They are *metamorphoo*: to change, real transformation of our minds and even our outward appearance, and *anakalupto*: open, unveiled, to uncover, once the veil is lifted it remains lifted forever. The veil is lifted from our eyes so that the Lord can correct us, change us, and prepare us to move forward and upward.

To simplify what Paul is saying to the Corinthians: If you Corinthians are going to move forward and upward into a greater glory, you must first make glorious the place where you are living and functioning right now. Only when your present state becomes glorious will God move you from glory to glory. This will require leaning on God for transformation or change of lifestyle to happen. Paul's words remain applicable to us today.

But how is one changed [*metamorphoo*]? We are changed by unveiling or opening our minds so that the Lord can change us. When we are "open" [looking into the mirror of God's Word], He can correct us. When the place we occupy becomes glorious then, and only then, can we move upward from glory to glory. The place where we are living right now must change before we can progress further. If we don't open our minds for spiritual growth, we will remain in the same unpleasant stage of our lives. It is the nature of God's creations to go through changes [*metamorphoo*]. An example of this fact is demonstrated in butterflies.

God loves every stage of our spiritual growth, but if we don't lean, we don't grow. He just doesn't want us to permanently remain in one stage. God loves butterflies, but he also loves caterpillars. However, caterpillars are not created to remain that way forever; they are to become butterflies. The intent of God is that all caterpillars change into butterflies. Many people see themselves as lowly caterpillars in a butterfly world. If you see yourself that way, you are not alone, but you don't have to remain that way. Unfortunately, the ten spies that Moses sent into the land of Canaan saw themselves as mere "grasshoppers" (low-life beings) compared to the giants who occupied the land. They said, ". . . we are as grasshoppers in our sight, and so we are in their [Canaanites'] sight" (Numbers 12:33) Ten of the twelve spies who went into Canaan to check it out saw only giants. It's amazing how contagious the lowly caterpillar-spirit can be. Two of the twelve spies, Joshua and Caleb, didn't let that spirit keep them from moving from glory to glory.

Do you feel like a caterpillar in a butterfly world? Most people feel that way at one time or other. There are stages that metamorphism goes through from an egg, to a caterpillar, to a cocoon, and then to a butterfly. To become a butterfly, you can't bypass the three previous stages. It takes time and patience to reach the final stage to be a beautiful, colorful, majestic butterfly. Spiritual growth is gradual as we gradually learn to lean on God.

Metamorphism is a natural process in caterpillars, but we have a free will, and if we change, we must choose to change. Spiritual growth takes deliberate, personal effort. Some people get stuck in the caterpillar stage and don't develop to their full potential. Others remain stuck in the cocoon stage and never break out, yet they are so close to becoming the butterfly that God gave them the ability to be. The secret is that once we choose, God gives us the grace to change and move to another level of His glory.

Our son Howie is writing a book entitled *How to be Number Two in a Number One World*. He served as an assistant pastor for several years. Now, he has become number one in leadership. His faithfulness in the number two position was necessary. He served cheerfully and faithfully, until he was recently promoted. He didn't stay in the caterpillar stage forever. None of us should and none of us have to.

A Worrisome Trend

Believe it or not, the new trend today is to partially lean on Jesus. People unashamedly advertise their new theology on coffee cups, T-shirts, and other merchandise that says, "I love Jesus, but _____." There should be no ifs, ands, or buts in a Christian's vocabulary. We can't say "Lord" and "no" in the same sentence.

This kind of thinking puts a person in the position of too good to go to hell, but not good enough to go to heaven. If you've ever flown on a commercial airline there is a status they call "standby" which means you are not assured of a seat, but if you have a ticket, you are assured of a seat. John the Beloved says salvation is an assurance ticket to heaven, not just a "standby" hoping you will get on the salvation plane. He says, "These things I have written to you who believe in the name of the Son of God, that you may know that you have eternal life, and that you may continue to believe in the name of the Son of God." (I John 5:13)

There will come a time in our lives when we will have no one to lean on but Jesus. Tragedy will come out of nowhere. Those are days when we don't feel like celebrating. It is during those times when we have only Jesus to lean on that we experience how much He cares for us. Leaning on God is not natural nor is it a gift. It's an experience. Life can be tough sometimes. So, what do we do? We can pray and trust the Word of God. We learn to lean on God and not on ourselves. We learn that we can't depend on our flesh to do the right thing, or depend on our wealth, or even our best friend. When Jesus needed help, He said, "My Father!" Cast self, pride, everything at the feet of Jesus and cry out to Him for help. And He will come; He is never far away. From being a follower of Jesus to becoming a disciple of Jesus is a continual learning process as we move from glory to glory.

Jeremiah (20:9) had bad days, too. He wanted to hide or just disappear. In fact, Jeremiah wished he had never been born (Jeremiah 20:18). Job was another Bible character who was severely tried, but he came out victorious. Carl Gustav Jung, a Swiss psychiatrist, wrote a book about Job's suffering entitled, *Answer to Job*. In it, he says that God sent his Son to die for man's sins because God realized that He had treated Job unjustly. According to Jung, God repented by sending His Son to die for His [God's] sins.[38] Let me be clear, God doesn't need to be forgiven because He cannot sin. We need to forgive God lest we have something against Him. Carl Jung had something against God, and instead of repenting, his contradiction of God was his book, *Answer to Job*.

> If your enemies can control who you say they are,
> they have already defeated you.

Jeremiah had his moments of frustration and was so disappointed that he compared God to a "wet spring." A wet spring is only reliable part of the time. God is not a wet spring, He is Jehovah-*SHAMMAH*; God is always "there." A wet spring is only wet during the rainy season but goes dry in the dry season when water is most needed. Jeremiah is saying that when he needed God the most, God was not there for him. He was mistaken. God is always there because He is Omnipresent. And He always "works all things together for the good to those who are called according to His purpose." (Romans 8:28)

Sometimes when we are overwhelmed with the cares of this life we need to get alone with God; then just let it go and sing praise songs to Him. Don't be like the wet spring in the example above because when it is a dry season there is no water [praise]. No matter how "dry" the present situation is in life, give God praise. We must learn to "serve the Lord with joy and gladness of heart for His abundance." (Deuteronomy 28:47)

When we feel God has let us down, and we have resentment in our hearts against Him, we must stop and repent; forgive God right now, not that He needs to be forgiven. We need to get things right between ourselves and God. Over the past half century, I have wanted to quit the ministry many times. Sometimes, I still must climb out from under the rubble and get on top of it and dance despite the dark days of depression. If we can muster the courage to face the rubble and climb on top of it by the grace of God, He will put a fire in us that the Adversary can't put out! Even in his discouragement Job said, "'Then I said, I will not make mention of Him, nor speak anymore in His name. But His word was in my heart like a burning fire shut up in my bones; I was weary of holding it back, And I could not." (Job 20:9) God's Word moved Job from discouragement to victory so that his rubble was under his feet and thereupon he danced.

Continue Leaning on God [A Word to Ministers]

In the Bible, birds are a symbol of freedom, and that is the message Jesus was teaching in Matthew 6:26: freedom from worry and anxiety. The Apostle Paul addressed the same subject about how to deal with anxiety in his letter to the Philippians 4:6, "Be anxious for nothing, but in everything by prayer and supplication with thanksgiving, let your requests be known to God."

Worry and anxiety are consumers. They will literally consume our health by causing high blood pressure, panic attacks, and even death. They will also consume our social and family lives, perhaps even to the destruction of a marriage. There are no benefits to worry and anxiety. So, then, how do we deal with them? We must make deliberate effort to choose not to be anxious or to worry, and we must also place complete trust in God for help with our problems.

When I was a pastor in my twenties, I found one way to deal with anxiety. I noticed that I was carrying my problems and concerns regarding my pastor duties home with me. I was especially anxious regarding those who were sick and/or dying. This is what I chose to do about it. When I returned home each day, I would pause at the door to my home and say to myself, out loud, 'I refuse to carry my worries and anxieties into my home and burden my family with them. I cast all my cares and concerns on You, Jesus." Then I would pause and visualize my burdens being placed on Christ. Thereafter, I would sense the peace of God, and I am sure my wife, Kaye, could also sense His peace. Isaiah said, ". . . the chastisement of our peace was laid on him." (Isaiah 53:5b) Try it; it works!

Speaking as a pastor for over fifty years myself, with half of those years in a denomination and the other half in an Independent church, I know generally what you face every day. We find it very difficult to return from a vacation refreshed and revived, ready to take the city for Christ, only to be met with the resignations of some of your top leadership. We are left with the decision to rebel, or resign, or start all over and rebuild. We decide to rebuild. We "gird up our loins" and try to encourage the others who are still with you to pick up the pieces and keep going forward.

Continue Leaning on God [A Word to Church Members]

Let me be the first to say that pastors are not perfect, and neither is pastoring a cushy job as it is often thought to be. That is why 80% of American pastors [4 out of 5] are discouraged in their ministry and suffer from depression and burnout. Our son is a pastor, and he works 60 to 70 hours a week, which is the average number of hours the majority of full-time pastors work per week. These hours include the time he spends as counselor, church administrator, in sermon preparation and, in our son's case, Chaplain of the city police department. And besides that, he is "on call" twenty-four hours each day for anyone who has a need, including a host of non-church members who number as many as the church membership.

There are two reasons why and how a pastor keeps his sanity: one is the call of God upon his life, and the other is the love and support of the loyal, faithful members who stick with him in spite of the hardships. The pastor who abuses his members for personal monetary gain and fails to love them with agape love [sacrificial love] will find himself answering to God on judgement day. The point I want to make is this. At first things may be difficult, but all that is difficult is not that way forever. Habakkuk learned this truth and it served him well because in the difficult times he learned to lean on God. My blessed mother learned this truth. When things would go wrong in her life, and a lot did for sure, she'd say, "Everything will be all right in the morning." She had attended numerous funerals in her lifetime, but in spite of her many losses, she had learned the joy of dancing on the rubble. You can do it too by God's wonderful grace.

My mother couldn't speak Hebrew, but if she could have spoken Hebrew, there is one expression she would have kept repeating, and that is "Shalom Aleichem-peace be to you." It means may you be blessed with prosperity, rest, safety, completion, wholeness, fullness, soundness, well-being and so much more. Jesus used that greeting when He appeared to His disciples behind closed and locked doors that were no barrier to the risen Lord and Savior. (John 20:19-22) Leaning on God means resting in His love.

Study Guide: Keep Leaning

Key Quote(s):
There are two little words that makes it possible to lean on God: "try" and "trust."

"Never be afraid to trust an unknown future to a known God." Corrie Ten Boom

Be careful when a naked man offers you a shirt. African saying

"Pray and let God worry." Martin Luther

Begin with Prayer
O, Father, my God, my Rock: attend to my cry as I lean on You today. When I am overwhelmed by life's pressure, lead me to the Rock that is higher than me. You are my everything. You are my refuge and strength. The strong tower that I run into for safety. I lean on You as I wait for you to provide an answer to my need. You are a Father to the fatherless and a defender of widows and orphans and Your ears are open to the cry of Your people all over this world. Make haste, O Father, to defend and comfort those who are persecuted for Your name's sake. I pray for my family, my church. I cry out for our nation and the nations of the world that they may come to know Your Son, Jesus Christ. Please send a worldwide revival and make me a part of it. I lean on You. "For thine is the kingdom, and the power, and the glory forever." In the righteous name of Jesus. Amen.

Book: Genesis

Author: Jewish tradition lists Moses as the author.

Date: Moses wrote Genesis around 1440 BC during the 40 years in the wilderness.

Inspiration: <u>Genesis 37</u>

² This is the history of Joseph. Joseph, being seventeen years old, was feeding the flock with his brother and Joseph brought a bad report of them to his father.

³ Now Israel loved Joseph more than all his children, because he was the son of his old age. Also, he made him a tunic of many colors.

⁴ But when his brothers saw that their father loved him more than all his brothers, they hated him and could not speak peaceably to him.

⁵ Now Joseph had a dream and he told it to his brothers, and they hated him even more.

¹⁸ Now when they saw him afar off, even before he came near them, they conspired against him to kill him.

¹⁹ Then they said to one another, "'Look, this dreamer is coming!'"

²⁰ "'Come therefore, let us now kill him and cast him into some pit; and we shall say, 'Some beast has devoured him.' We shall see what will become of his dreams.'"

²⁸ Then Midianite traders passed by; so, the brothers pulled Joseph up and lifted him out of the pit and sold him to the Ishmaelites for twenty shekels of silver. And they took Joseph to Egypt.

<u>Genesis 39</u>

¹⁻² Now Joseph had been taken down to Egypt. And Potiphar, an officer of Pharaoh, captain of the guard, an Egyptian, bought him from the Ishmaelites who had taken him down there. The Lord was with Joseph, and he was a successful man; and he was in the house of his master the Egyptian.

⁷⁻⁹ And it came to pass after these things that his master's wife cast longing eyes on Joseph, and she said lie with me. But he refused and said to his master's wife, "'Look, my master does not know what is with me in the house, and he has committed all that he has to my hand. There is no one greater in this house than I, nor has he kept back anything from me but you, because you are his wife. How then can I do this great wickedness, and sin against God?'"

¹¹⁻¹² But it happened about this time, when Joseph went into the house to do his work, and none of the men of the house was inside. That she caught him by his garments, saying, "'Lie with me.'" But he left his garment in her hand and fled and ran outside.

[16] So she kept his garment with her until his master came home.

[19-20a] So, it was, when his master heard the words which his wife spoke to him, saying. "Your servant did to me after this manner," that his anger was aroused. Then Joseph's master took him and put him into the prison.

[21-22] But the Lord was with Joseph and showed him mercy, and He gave him favor in the sight of the keeper of the prison. And the keeper of the prison committed to Joseph's hand all the prisoners who were in the prison; whatever they did there, it was his doing.

Genesis 40

[1,3] It came to pass after these things, that the butler and the baker of the king of Egypt offended their lord, the king of Egypt. So, he put them in custody in the house of the captain of the guard, in the prison the place where Joseph was confined.

For the rest of Joseph's story, read chapters 41 through 50.

Backstory

The story of Joseph in the Old Testament is one of my favorites because I feel a "kindred spirit" to him. Not because I had similar experiences, but because I can relate to the divine call on his life. Joseph's story is found in Genesis: 37-50. He was the first son born to Jacob and Rachel, Jacob's true love. Jacob showed special favor to Joseph with a coat of "many colors" that many believed was a long robe with long sleeves that indicated royalty. That could be why his brothers were jealous of him.

When he was 17 years-old, his brothers sold him into slavery which landed him in Egypt where he spent the remainder of his life. When he was sold into slavery, his life took a major detour and looked a lot different in the end. I can relate to the last part because my life turned out differently from the way it began. However, there is one thing I can relate to that Joseph experienced and that is pain. Ironically, that was the key to his success.

Charles Swindoll labels Joseph as a man of "integrity and forgiveness." Joseph was coddled as a child by his father Jacob. Now in Egypt, those days were over. Potiphar, an officer of Pharaoh, a captain of the guard who was an Egyptian, bought him from the Ishmaelites. Potiphar made Joseph overseer of his house and God blessed and prospered everything that Joseph touched. Potiphar's wife lied about Joseph and he was thrown in prison. Even though he was wrongfully charged he didn't hold any grudges or sit in the corner of the prison cell sulking and complaining. He allowed his gift which was administration or management to continue to work in his life.

He became in charge of the king's prison. He met the king's baker and cupbearer who were prisoners. Joseph could have treated them badly out of anger for what had been done to him, but instead he treated them with respect. Both men had dreams and Joseph interpreted the dreams for them. He could have told them to "bug off and not bother him" but he didn't do it. He listened to them. He helped them in spite of his own problems. (Genesis 4:5-7) Joseph told the cupbearer to remember him when he was restored to the king's favor, but he forgot him. Joseph remained in prison for two more years. During his dozen or more years in prison he grew closer to God in faith and trust.

The cupbearer finally remembered Joseph when the king needed someone to interpret the king's dream of prosperity and famine. Joseph interpreted the king's dream and Pharaoh's officials began a search for a person who could do the job. (Genesis 41:37-38) Joseph was put in charge of Egypt's food supply. (Gen. 41:33) Joseph didn't volunteer. He kept quiet and let God promote him. In one day, Joseph was released from prison, but we must not lose sight of the fact that Joseph waited patiently for two years before this "one day" came, and he was put in a place of authority.

Joseph brought glory to God and not to himself. (Genesis 41: 39-41) He was a man who leaned on God with all his might. He was a man of integrity, patience, and character. He never lost sight of his heritage or God's covenant with Abraham regarding Israel. He showed love toward his family and even his brothers who sold him into slavery. His only request was that his remains be carried back home to Israel when he died. (Genesis 50:25) Moses honored his request and took Joseph's bones with him in the exodus. (Exodus 13:19)

When you are treated unfairly, and you need someone to lean on refer to Joseph as a great example of how to lean on God and trust His perfect timing. And yes, dance on the rubble!

Personal Application: Prayerfully write down your answers to the following questions.

1. In your own words, what do you think was going through Joseph's mind when his brothers sold him into slavery?

2. What do you believe enabled Joseph, at such a young age, to lean on God?

3. What did Joseph's "coat of many colors" represent?

4. There are two little words that make it possible to lean on God. What are they?
   a.

   b.

Read Ahead (small group): Read chapter 7: Keep Letting Go
Below is a space for you to write any insights you might have from reading Chapter 7.

_____

_____

_____

Take this Survey

Ranking yourself from 1 to 10, how satisfied are you with your leaning on Jesus? 1 being "I seldom lean" and 10 being "I lean a lot." Circle one number.

1   2   3   4   5   6   7   8   9   10

Comments _____

_____

Essential References: I Peter 5:7; Philippians 4:6-7; Proverbs 4:25-27; Isaiah 26:3; Colossians 3:2; Proverbs 3:5; Philippians 3:13-14.

Chapter 7

Keep Letting Go

One of the most important decisions we can make in life is to be willing to let go of our baggage. We collect our baggage from our own particular circumstances in life. Baggage is anything detrimental to us; that is, it can be physical, spiritual, emotional, or psychological.

Unhealthy Baggage:

- lust
- pride
- self-blame
- shame
- unforgiveness
- jealousy
- guilt
- legalism
- control
- stubbornness

> It is spiritual slavery to hold on to things that have no place or purpose in our lives.

This is in no way an inclusive list. Can you think of others from your personal experience?

Note them below:

_____

_____

_____

John the Beloved divided unhealthy baggage into three different categories. Simply stated, there are three temptations to sin that every human being will experience in his or her lifetime. The temptations are referred to in Scripture as the works of the flesh. John writes: "For all that is in the world—the **lust of the flesh**, the **lust of the eyes**, and the **pride of life**—is not of the Father but of the world." (John 2:15)

Unhealthy Baggage Defined

1. The **lust of the flesh** is that temptation to pursue physical satisfactions such as sex, pornography, physical violence, drugs, (marijuana, alcohol, opioids, pills) and so much more.
2. **Lust of the eyes** is the temptation to look upon something we should not look upon, to cast eyes upon something with desire, even though God has told us not to look upon these things. A good example is King David. He was a married man who from his rooftop watched Bathsheba , a married woman, bathing. David was consumed with lust, and his actions resulted in an adulterous sexual relationship, a murdered husband, and an illegitimate son. (II Samuel 11:2-17)
3. The **pride of life** is only mentioned one time in the Bible. (I John 2:16) It is linked to the lust of the eyes. The pride of life is ego-centered and filled with self-importance. The story in Luke 18:10-14 is a clear example of what pride is. Two men went up to the temple to pray, a Publican [tax collector] and a Pharisee [religious leader]. Simply put, the Publican humbled himself and repented of his sins, but the Pharisee spent his time praising his own good deeds.

Discarding Unhealthy Baggage

It is necessary to identify the works of the flesh to help us discover more deeply how we can effectively battle against our human nature by letting go and allowing the Holy Spirit to mirror the nature of Christ in us. To accomplish this, we must live in the fruit of the Spirit. The fruit of the Spirit is contrasted with the works of the flesh. Notice that Paul says "fruit" [singular]. He is not naming nine different kinds of fruit that the Spirit gives. Instead, he is describing the characteristics of the fruit that God's grace and the Holy Spirit is working in us. The list below is not just to identify the fruit of the Spirit, but also to allow the grace of God to put the fruit into action in our lives.

What Baggage Is Not

Love — I John 4:16; I Corinthians 1:4-8
Joy — Nehemiah 8:10
Peace — Romans 5:1
Longsuffering — Colossians 1:11
Gentleness — Ephesians 4:2
Goodness — Ephesians 5:9
Meekness — Matthew 5:5
Faith — Ephesians 3:16-17
Self-control — 2 Peter 1:5-7

The Apostle Paul was victorious over the lust of the flesh, lust of the eyes, and pride of life because he actively demonstrated the fruit of the Spirit. When we read Paul's thirteen New Testament epistles [letters] that he wrote to the churches, he encourages them to "fight a good fight, finish the race, and keep the faith." (2 Timothy 4:7-8) Even though Paul admonished the churches at times, he also encouraged them to be faithful in these three things.

Fighting a Good Fight

Paul said that he had fought a good fight, but what did he mean when he said that? For a fight to be a good fight, it must be regulated by a set of Godly rules; although, the battle is not physical but spiritual. (Ephesians 6:12) Ephesians was Paul's last epistle before he was martyred around 67 AD. He uses the Greek word *agonizomai*, translated "fought" to describe what he meant by "I have fought a good fight." The word means "to engage in conflict." Enough cannot be said about Paul's struggles against evil. His battle was not with flesh and blood, and neither is our battle with flesh and blood, but with Satan himself. (Ephesians 6:12) Take the time to read 2 Corinthians 11:23-33 to catch a glimpse of the battles Paul fought and the unbelievable struggles he went through to accomplish his mission to preach Christ to an unsaved world.

It may be easier for us to let go of material things when we remember that Jesus was tempted in all manners as we human beings are. (Hebrews 4:15) Jesus understands every weakness of ours because he was tempted in the ways we are, but He did not sin. It is true that some things are more difficult to let go of than others. Even though some issues are more difficult to deal with than others, we must be willing to submit ourselves to the will of God and let go of them.

It is spiritual slavery to hold on to things that have no place or purpose in our lives. To make a difference, we must let go those behaviors that hinder our becoming like our Lord who prays for us to overcome the temptations of the lust of the flesh, lust of the eyes, and pride of life. To accomplish these goals, we have to make some hard, but rewarding, choices. As we can see, letting go and eliminating the unhealthy baggage from our lives will also take time, but it will always be left up to us to make the choice.

Choice
God cannot not know everything,
but He can choose not to know
everything.

God cannot not be everywhere,
but He can choose not to be
everywhere.

God cannot not be all powerful,
but He can choose not to be
all powerful.

Choice is the essence of God's perfection.
He made man in His own image, and
gifted him with part of himself:
the ability to choose.
--Roy H. Cantrell

When I think of letting go of our material and emotional baggage, two images come to mind. The first image is that of a man inside of a giant hot air balloon. The balloon can't rise because it is tethered to earth, and it has too much weight inside of it. If he doesn't untether the balloon and cast the added weights overboard, he will not be able to rise upward. Spectators yell to him, "Untether the balloon!" He can't hear them yelling over the roar of the hot air bellowing into the balloon above him. The balloon represents life as we know it. The balloon is tethered to earth by long ropes or cables that are untied when the balloon is launched. Inside the gondola, or basket, may be luggage and weights that must be thrown out to rise off the ground and in case of emergency to give the balloon the added lift it will need to get over a barrier that lies in its path. Life is like a hot air balloon because it is tethered to the material stuff of this world and when our lives are ready to launch, they have to be untethered so that we, too, can rise heavenward one day. To successfully make that eventful journey it will require us to lighten the load by "letting go" of earthly ties and baggage that we hold dear to our hearts.

The second image of letting go is the method by which monkeys are captured with the least harm being done to them. A hole is made in a coconut just large enough for a monkey to squeeze its paw into. Two smaller holes are made in the top to thread a stout string or wire through them to secure the coconut to the tree limb. A piece of banana is placed inside of the coconut to lure the monkey. The trap is set. The monkey smells the fruit, reaches inside, grasps the piece of banana making a fist that is larger than the hole into which he put his paw. Alas, the monkey is trapped, but only because he won't let go.

We quickly condemn the monkey for being so foolish for holding on to something as small as a piece of banana and the man for not untethering the balloon. However, aren't we also as stubborn sometimes when we hold on to temporal things that jeopardize our eternal future? Eve held on to a bite of fruit that cost her and all humanity eternal life. And again, let's not be foolhardy to judge Eve for what she did because how many times have we yielded to temptation and held on to something which we should have let go? The good news is God sent His only Son, Jesus, to set us free if we trust Him and are willing to let go of our baggage.

Keeping the Faith

The general definition of keeping the faith is to continue to believe in, trust, or support someone or something when it is difficult to do so. Biblically speaking, keeping the faith requires a love for the truth which is the Word of God. Moses wrote about the importance of teaching the faith to the children. (Deuteronomy 4:9) John explains that we can trust the Holy Spirit to lead us in all truth (John 16:13), and the apostle Paul gives numerous warnings of some people who would abandon the faith and accept another gospel. (I Timothy 4:1; Galatians 1:6-7) He wrote how critical it was to keep the faith saying that those who ignored his advice "have suffered shipwreck" regarding their faith. (I Timothy 1:19)

As you read this, there are millions of Christians who are suffering intimidation, persecution, and death for their faith. Their churches are being destroyed, and some members of their congregation while worshipping in church are being martyred by terrorists for their faith. It is not an overstatement to say it will cost us everything to keep the faith. It requires love of and strong commitment to God and His Word that won't yield to any and all attacks for being a believer.

Finishing the Race

Some may feel that ending this book on finishing the race with an emphasis on death and dying may be depressing, but it was not so in the opinion of the Apostle Paul and a myriad of others. Take the time to read Tony and Ann Jett's testimony of their struggle with the death of their son, Matthew in **Others Who Have Danced on the Rubble** section in the back of this book.

What did Paul mean when he said, "I have finished the race?" When on the cross Jesus said, "It is finished" the Greek word used is *tetelestai* which means "to bring to a close, to complete, to fulfill." Much of the significance of the meaning of the Greek is lost when translated into English. The full meaning of the word is "to continue to be finished." "It was finished for that moment and for all time. This is so important because it indicates a condition, a state of being, a resting place. It indicates the ongoing nature of our salvation."

When Paul said, "I have finished the race," he meant that his work was finished for that moment as well as for all time. Although death was near for him, he rested in the "continuing" assurance of his salvation that he would rest in the presence of God forever.

As children bring their broken toys
With fears for us to mend
I brought my broken dreams to God
Because He was my friend.

But then instead of leaving Him
In peace to work alone
I stayed around and tried to help
Through ways that were my own.

At last I snatched them back and cried,
"How can you be so slow?"
"My child," He said,
"What could I do? You never did let go."
Author Unknown

The longer I live, the more I think about this: our Christian lives hinge on our love for God and each other. We either practice love, or we don't. Since the Word says love one another, we had better do it. When we come to the end of our lives, love is the one thing we don't lose. It is the one and only thing we can take with us to heaven. All that you have done for Christ is sent on ahead.

A rose is the symbol of love, and love is always personal, it is a life-and-death matter. Without love, people die. There is nothing worse than to be alone and not be loved. I believe that the world suffers mostly, not from food hunger, but from love hunger. If we have love, we will feed those hungry for food. When George Matheson, the blind preacher, died he was honored by those who put red roses in his grave. It was done in honor of his dedicated life of love for God and the people. Perhaps you will recall the poem Matheson wrote.

"O Love that will not let me go,
I rest my weary soul in Thee.
I give Thee back the life I owe,
That in Thine ocean depths it flows
May richer, fuller be."

When we trust Christ for our salvation, we are trusting God's love for us. The love of God will cause us to place our hands in His. When my children were small and when we crossed the street, I held their hands until we got to the other side. Trusting Christ is simply the act of placing our hands in His and trusting Him completely to see us safely to the other side. Jude put it this way: "Now unto him who is able to keep you from falling. And to present you faultless before the presence of His glory with exceeding joy. To the all wise God, our Savior, be glory, majesty, dominion and power, both now and forever. Amen" (Jude 24, 25) Trusting Christ is letting go and letting God do the rest.

The following list is short and certainly not complete or inclusive, it contains some of the things we should let go in our lives. The list is presented in no specific order of importance. They are all important.

- ➢ Let go of the past and concerns for the present and future
- ➢ Let go of guilt
- ➢ Let go of pride
- ➢ Let go of stubbornness
- ➢ Let go of legalism
- ➢ Let go of control
- ➢ Let go of offense
- ➢ Let go of insecurities
- ➢ Let go of blame
- ➢ Let go of unhealthy habits
- ➢ Let go of shame

The only way we can dance on the rubble is to LET GO of those things that we are holding on to that are hindering our spiritual walk with God. If we will let go and trust Christ, He will fill the void.

Finally, the word chosen by the Holy Spirit for the picture perfect, shared indwelling of the Trinity is *perichoresis.* It literally means "dancing around." In her book entitled *Christmas Dance*, author Kay Horner says, "*Perichoresis* is the theological term used by the early church fathers to describe the oneness or interpersonal communion. A combination of two Greek words simply meaning 'to give way' or 'to make room,' it could also be translated to mean 'rotation' or 'a going around.' Consequently, some have compared this divine interplay to a dance. If we express our joy and happiness on earth by dancing, when we reach heaven we will run, jump, and dance, but it won't be on the rubble of our lives. It will be on streets of gold!"

The End of Satan

Dr. David Jeremiah relates a story by Carolyn Arends in his book *Agents of the Apocalypse."* Carolyn said that she enjoyed "Mission Sunday" in her church, especially when missionaries came and spoke to them. She tells about a time when a young couple came and told them about an incident when an enormous boa constrictor snake, much larger than a man, came through the front door into the kitchen. The couple ran out of the house and found a native who came and chopped off the snake's head with a machete. Afterward, he came out and warned the couple not to go back into the house because it would take some time before the snake would realize it was dead.

When Jesus died on the cross, He effectively cut off Satan's head (Genesis 3:15). Satan just hasn't realized it yet. The snake in the story was still a threat, although it was headless. The death, burial, and resurrection of Christ ended Satan's life span and ultimately limited his power over the kingdom of God.

[We Are] Not Home Yet

I recall hearing about a missionary who came home on a furlough. She arrived in the U.S. on a large ship to a huge cheering crowd with signs that read "Welcome Home!" She was elated until she found out that a celebrity was on board and the people were cheering that person. She was disappointed and asked God why there was not a welcoming group there for her. God's word to her was, "You are not home yet."

The story touched me because I have never felt at home anywhere I have lived. It is not because I haven't lived in nice homes or lovely cities, because I have. I was raised poor and lived in log cabins in my early childhood, but later in life I have been privileged to live in some beautiful homes. I have searched for the reason why I don't feel at home in this world. I have moved a lot in my lifetime. To be exact, I have counted the number to be at least twenty-five. My father was an alcoholic, and when he was drunk, we might move on a whim. But I don't think the many moves is the reason why I don't feel at home in this world. It is because this world is not my home; I am just passing through.

I believe there is an emptiness in all who are God's children who desire to be with their heavenly Father someday and that longing will never leave until that happens. I believe the story of the prodigal son is an example of how a son got tired of his worldly lifestyle and wanted to come home. The father in the story exemplifies our heavenly Father welcoming us home to be with Him forever.

I believe all who know Jesus as their Savior will never feel at home in this world because this world is not our final destination. We are not home yet! That is why this lesson is so important because LETTING GO is a natural instinct for every Christian to prepare for the final move to their final home for a welcome home celebration that will be out of this world.

Heaven Is My Home

Shortly after I finished *Dancing on the Rubble,* I purchased Jonathan Kahn's latest book titled: *The Oracle*. When I read his final remarks, I was surprised that he and I had used a similar illustration and scripture to close. I'm including his closing because he nailed it. Here is an excerpt from Jonathan Kahn's closing.

Tell me, said the Oracle." "Why is it that you never feel at home!"

"At home where?"

"In this world . . ."

"Did you ever think it strange?" he asked, "to spend your entire life in this world, to know nothing else but this world...and yet to never feel at home within it?"

"Why is that?"

"Because it isn't home."[39]

Some of the last words of comfort that Jesus spoke to His disciples were that He was going to prepare a place for them and for everyone who accepted Jesus as his or her personal Savior. Jesus said, "In my Father's house are many mansions. . . . I go to prepare a place for you. . . . I will come again and receive you to myself that where I am you may be also." (John 14)

This promise from Jesus is indelibly imprinted on every human being's conscience. It is put there by God Himself, and that is why every person can never and will never feel at home in this world. Every human being comes into this world looking for someone who is looking for them. Jesus is the One who is looking for us, and we are looking for Him though we may not even know it. Jesus came to find and to save those who are lost. He will search until He finds us. And when He finds us, we will find Him and accept Him as our personal Savior. We will never feel content in this world anymore. Jesus said, "and you shall seek me and find me if you search for me with all your heart." (Jeremiah 29:13) We search for God until He finds us.

There is no human voice that we remember so clearly than that of a mother or father. It often seems that we can even hear those voices in our minds long after they can no longer speak to us. When God speaks to our hearts and minds, we will recognize His voice. When He does call our name, we will know it is Him. It may or may not be an audible voice, but we will know it is Him calling us to repent and receive Him as our Lord and Savior. If you don't know Jesus as your personal Savior, He is calling your name right now.

Nothing is an accident. You didn't accidently read this book. If you are not a Christian, turn to the "ABC's of Salvation" section in the back of this book and you will find information on how to become one.

Just let go! Dance on the rubble for the time will come when we will dance on streets of gold [Heaven] in a city with walls of jasper and gates of pearl!

Study Guide: Keep Letting Go

Key Quote(s):
"All the art of living lies in a fine mingling of letting go and hanging on."
H. Havelock Ellis

It hurts to let go, but sometimes it hurts more to hold on.

Eternity lasts forever but stuff doesn't.

"Brethren, I do not count myself to have apprehended (laid hold of it), but one thing I do, forgetting those things which are behind and reaching forward to those things which are ahead. I press toward the goal for the prize of the upward call of God in Christ Jesus." (Philippians 3:13-14)

"Therefore, we also, since we are surrounded by so great a cloud of witnesses, let us lay aside every weight, and the sin which so easily ensnares us, and let us run with endurance the race that is set before us. Looking unto Jesus" (Hebrews 12:1-2a)

One of the hardest things to do in life is letting go of what you think is real or true.

"There are two ways to be fooled. One is to believe what isn't true. The other is to refuse to accept what is true." Soren Kierkegaard

Letting go can be the most difficult thing you can do in life.

Begin with Prayer
O God, my Savior who won't let me go. My heart is steadfast in You. I praise You with my whole heart for great things You have done. My desire is to be with You and only You now and forever. If there be any wicked way in me, I ask now for forgiveness. Give me the grace and I will let go of anything and everything that will separate me from Your favor and holy presence. If You had not been with me when I faced my enemies who rose up against me, I would have been swallowed and eaten alive, but You prevailed against them and saved me out of all my

troubles. Your blessings are upon me, I sense it and know it even now. My heart is steadfast, my heart is steadfast, O God. Help me to let go of the wisdom of this world and cling to only You that You may be exalted in my life. In the righteous name of Jesus. Amen.

Author: The Apostle Paul

Date: 55 or 56 A D

Inspiration: II Corinthians 11:22-33

[22] "Are they Hebrews? So am I. Are they the seed of Abraham? So am I.

[23] Are they ministers of Christ? —I speak as a fool—I am more: In labors more abundant, in stripes above measure, prisons more frequently, in death often.

[24] From the Jews five times I received forty stripes minus one.

[25] Three times I was beaten with rods; once I was stoned; three times I was ship wrecked; a night and a day I have been in the deep;

[26] In journeys often, in perils of waters, in perils of robbers, in perils of my own countrymen, in perils of the Gentiles, in perils in the city, in perils in the wilderness, in perils in the sea, in perils among the brethren.

[27] In weariness and toil, in sleeplessness often, in hunger and thirst, in fasting often, in cold and nakedness—

[28] Besides the other things, what comes upon me daily: my deep concern for all the churches?

[29] Who is weak? Am not I weak? Who is made to stumble, and I do not burn with indignation?

[30] If I must boast, I will boast in the things which concern my infirmity.

[31] The God and Father of our Lord Jesus Christ, who is blessed forever, know that I am not lying.

[32] In Damascus the governor, under Aretas the king, was guarding the city of the Damascenes with a garrison, desiring to arrest me;

[33] But I was let down in a basket through a window in the wall and escaped from his hands.

Chapter 12:1-10

[1] It is doubtless not profitable for me to boast. I will come to visions and revelations of the Lord:

² I know a man in Christ who fourteen years ago—whether in the body I do not know, or whether out of the body I do not know, God knows—such a one was caught up to the third heaven.

³ And I know such a man—whether in the body or out of the body I do not know, God knows—

⁴ How he was caught up into Paradise and heard inexpressible words, which it is not lawful for a man to utter.

⁵ Of such a one I will boast; yet of myself I will not boast, except in my infirmities [plural].

⁶ For though I might desire to boast, I will not be a fool; for I will speak the truth. But I refrain, lest anyone should think of me above what he sees me to be or hears from me.

⁷ And lest I should be exalted above measure by the abundance of the revelations, a thorn in the flesh was given to me, a messenger of Satan to buffet me, lest I be exalted above measure.

⁸ Concerning this thing I pleaded with the Lord three times that it [singular] might depart from me.

⁹ And He said to me, "My grace is sufficient for you, for my strength is make perfect in weakness." Therefore, most gladly I will rather boast in my infirmities (Plural), that the power of Christ may rest upon me.

¹⁰ Therefore I take pleasure in infirmities, in reproaches, in needs, in persecutions, in distresses, for Christ's sake. For when I am weak, then I am strong.

Backstory

Here are some interesting facts about Paul and his relationship with the Corinthian church:

- Paul founded the church at Corinth in 50 A.D. sometime during his 18 months visit there. (Acts 18)
- Paul wrote second Corinthians from Macedonia on his way back to Corinth again in 55 or 56 AD to settle a dispute over Paul's apostolic authority.
- Second Corinthians is autobiographical and contains numerous references to the many sufferings and difficulties Paul had been through. He had radically decided to let go of all personal ambitions and serve the Lord. He wasn't about to let some faction in

the Corinthian church destroy it. Not if he could help it.

- This letter to the Corinthians serves as an invaluable guide in examining our own motivations for serving the Lord. Paul loved the church that he once persecuted and was willing to pay any cost to preserve it. Paul let go of his flawed theology when he was struck down by God on the road to Damascus and he was determined that those at Corinth were not going to pollute God's Word. He defended his ministry with a spirit of love and compassion for the people in the Corinthian church, but also with an uncompromising loyalty to the Word of God. And so should we.
- Paul's fear was not that the Corinthian church would be dissolved, but his fear was that it would survive without God in it. The thought that I could settle for belonging to a church where God once was troubles me and every believer. Think about it.

The Apostle Paul was in a spiritual race and so are we. He compared the Christian life to an Olympic race of his day. The runner kept his eye on the goal line and pressed toward the goal with all his might. The writer of Hebrew says, ". . . let us lay aside every weight, and the sin which so easily ensnares us, and let us run with endurance the race that is set before us. . . . Looking unto Jesus, the author and finisher of our faith, who for the joy that was set before Him endured the cross, despising the shame, and has sat down at the right hand of the throne of God" (Hebrews 12:1-2) we should lay aside every weight and sin that entangles us in worldly affairs.

Paul compared the struggles of a spiritual race to a physical race. As the Olympian runner looked toward the goal line for inspiration, Paul admonished the Christian to look unto Jesus, the author and finisher of their faith for inspiration. We too must keep our eyes on Jesus and look to him for strength to finish the race that we are running. God is the only one who stands beside us at the starting line, and the only one who can cross the finish line with us!

I'm sure you saw on television recently when runners showed acts of kindness during a race. They stopped to assist a competitor who had fallen. They were not satisfied with just winning and crossing the finish line alone. Neither should we be. This spiritual race we Christians are running must not be a race that we are just willing to win. We are duty-bound to pick someone up who has fallen and take them with us. I don't want to hear Jesus say to me when I get to heaven: "Roy, why did you come alone?"

The Hebrew writer uses the word "looking": *aphorao* (af-or-ah-oh): Strong's # 872: From *apo*, "away from." and *horao*, "to see." The word signifies undivided attention, looking away from all distractions in order to fix one's gaze on one object. *Aphorao* in Hebrews 12:2 means "having eyes for no one but Jesus."'

The word *aphorao* does not imply that we are not to be concerned about those around us. Jesus said to His disciples, after witnessing to the woman at the well, "Do you not say, 'There are four months and then comes the harvest'? Behold, I say to you, lift up your eyes and look at the fields, for they are already white for harvest."

The statement "there are four months and then comes the harvest," was probably a saying that meant that there was no real rush to harvest. An excuse basically, not to get into a hurry to harvest of souls. Therefore, Jesus brought it to the disciple's attention that "the fields were white for harvest" (probably pointing to the people who were coming from the town of Samaria). Following the conversation that Jesus had with the woman, the Bible says, "The woman then left her water pot, went her way into the city, and said to the men, 'Come, see a Man who told me all things that I ever did. Could this be the Christ?'"

Jesus was not a condemner but a forgiver. He didn't shame; He claimed. Jesus said to the Samaritan woman, "Neither do I condemn you." Jesus forgave her, a woman rejected by a religious society. She led a whole city to come and see and hear Christ. I've never done that. When we are seated at the Marriage Supper of the Lamb Look across the table she will be there probably near Jesus.

> "Let God have your life; He can do more with it than you can." D. L. Moody

---

Near the end of his life, Paul ended his letter to Timothy in which he said three things that he had done:

- "I have fought the good fight,
- I have finished the race,
- I have kept the faith."

The only way we can dance on the rubble is to LET GO of the things that are holding us back or weighing us down and hindering our spiritual journey. If we will let go and let God lead us, He will fill the void in our lives. If we will check our life's baggage, we will find junk inside that we won't believe we have kept this long and that we don't need. We have held on to "stuff" for years, things that we have forgotten about. That is why the Bible says to "lay aside every weight and the sin that so easily clings to you." "Examine yourself as to whether you are in the faith. Test yourselves, do you not know yourselves, that Jesus Christ is in you? Unless you are disqualified [do not stand the test]." II Corinthians 13:5

Occasionally, Kaye will buy a new purse, or change to another purse she already has, so she dumps everything out of the other purse into the one she plans to use. Honestly, when she dumps everything from her purse to put into the next one, I am amazed how much she can get into one medium size purse. Everything from postage stamps and hand sanitizer to scissors.

Periodically we, too, need to check our spiritual luggage and LET GO of baggage we have held on to that is taking up good space in our spiritual walk. So, take the time right now to take inventory of your past and present in light of your eternity, keep what is good and throw away the "stuff" you don't need. Shake it off! Let it go! You will be dancing on the "rubble" before you know it.

Redeem the Time! Why?

Paul admonished his spiritual son Timothy to "redeem the time because the days are evil." (Ephesians 5:16) But what did he mean by this advice? He was saying, buy up every opportunity and make the most of your life and make it count for the glory of God because life will end someday. And you must give an account for how you use every second of your life. He was saying, "My work here on earth is finished. It's over!" and he knew his departure was near.

How did Paul make it to the finish line? When he said, "I have finished the race." It's the same awareness Jesus uttered on the Cross when He said, "It is finished" (Greek word: *etelestai* meaning "paid in full.")

> "Letting go and letting God begins where
> the will of God is known." Roy Cantrell

I believe the Holy Spirit will give us a sense of knowing when our purpose in this life is fulfilled. He will give us spiritual eyes to see when we are near the finish line. That's why we must not let things of this life distract us, but instead "looking unto Jesus" the author and finisher of our faith. That's way we must "fight, finish and keep the faith," until we cross our finish line. When our finish line is in sight, we must put every ounce of our strength into overdrive, turn on the after burners, share Jesus with one more person, and finish strong. Then shout, "Hallelujah it is finished; I'm going home!"

Personal Application: Prayerfully write down your answers to the following questions.

1. What do you think Paul meant when he said, "I take pleasure in my infirmities?"

2. What were some of the accusations Paul received from people around him?
    *The Jews?

    *The Gentiles?

    * False Apostles

    * Roman government?

3. Paul's greatest obstacle was the "thorn in the flesh." What is yours?

4. In what way can you relate, or not relate, to the Apostle Paul?

Comments _____
_____
_____
_____

Take this Survey
Ranking yourself from 1 to 10: "How satisfied are you with "letting go?"
1 being "I can't let go" and 10 "I can let go." Circle one number.

1   2   3   4   5   6   7   8   9   10

Comments _____
_____

   Essential References: Ephesians 4:31-32; Philippians. 3:13-14; Isaiah 43:18-19; I Corinthians 9:24; Romans 8:26; I Peter 5:7; Philippians 4:6; Proverbs 28:13; Hebrews 12:1-2; Ephesians 4:26-27.

Let go of your past so that God can do something with your future.

The End

Don't criticize what you don't understand. Michal (David's wife) was critical of King David's actions because they weren't the norm. I have been guilty of the same thing. We can miss a lot of blessings by being too quick to speak against something we don't understand. It is okay to question everything but be careful that you aren't quick to speak against something until you have given it a lot of thought and prayer. There are dire circumstances for anyone who fights against God's doings. Saul, who later took the name Paul, found out on the road to Damascus when he ran squarely into God and was struck with blindness. Michal also suffered for her words of condemnation toward her husband David when she criticized him for dancing and playing music before the Lord. "Therefore, Michal the daughter of [King] Saul, had no children to the days of her death." (II Samuel 6:23)

There are always critics who will condemn others for the slightest sign of outward expression of happiness or joy. Christians ought to be the happiest people in the world. But, too often they are known for their downcast faces and stringent lifestyle. I hope this book has given you a reason to rejoice rather than live your life depressed and defeated. I have found that critical people are among those who suffer the most from depression. *Sow Joy: It's a Choice* is a book of poetry I wrote amidst some of my worst trials. It is amazing how some of the best God has for us can come during our worst and darkest hours. Stop right here and bless the Lord God, King of the Universe.

The Devil Wants to Keep You Quiet

Remember, I mentioned previously how my parents told us children, "If you laugh, you will cry." Their purpose for saying this was to keep us quiet. But as harmless as it seemed to our parents, it had a negative effect because it took the very life out of us. The Bible says, "This is the day that the Lord has made, rejoice and be glad in it."(Psalm 118:24) Being raised in a home with an alcoholic father (*Scars and Stripes: Hope for Adult Children of Alcoholic Families*), we needed all the laughter we could get just to survive. Take away the laughter and it is like depriving a plant of water; it will wilt and die. Only Jesus can restore joy through his blood in the New Covenant of salvation regardless of life's circumstances. And the ultimate joy will be when we raise our cup with Him in celebration at the Marriage Supper of the Lamb. We will dance on the rubble of Satan's ultimate defeat, which will rival any dancing with the stars on earth because we will be dancing among the stars of the universe forever. Therefore, we should be more determined than ever to press on without compromise. Repeat the following prayer:

Giver of life, creator of all that is lovely,
Teach me to sing the words of your song;
I want to feel the music of living
And not fear the sad songs
But from them make new songs
Composed of both laughter and tears.
Teach me to dance to the sounds of your world
And your people,
I want to move in rhythm with your plan,
Help me to try to follow your leading
To risk even falling
To rise and keep trying
Because you are leading the dance.

Author Unknown

"Life can be counted on to provide
all the pain that any of us might need."

Sheldon Kopp from
Joni Eareckson Tada's Website

Sister Anne Shields

"I am finished with low living, sight walking, small planning, smooth knees, colorless dreams, tamed visions, mundane talking, frivolous, living, selfish giving, and dwarfed goals. I lean on Christ's presence. I love with patience, live by prayer, and labor with the power of God's grace. My face is set. My gate is fast, my goal is heaven. My road is narrow, my way is rough, my companions are few, my guide is reliable, and my mission is clear. I cannot be bought, compromised, detoured, lured away, turned back deluded, or delayed. I will not flinch in the face of sacrifice, hesitate in the presence of adversity, negotiate at the table of the enemy, ponder at the pool of popularity, or meander in the maze of mediocrity. I won't give up, shut up, let up, stored up, prayed up, paid up, and spoken up for the cause of Christ. I am a disciple."

> We're never perfect, but good enough!
> Never mark your mistakes.

Changing Direction

On New Year's Day 1929, Georgia Tech played UCLA in the Rose Bowl. In that game, a young man named Roy Riegels recovered a fumble for UCLA. Picking up the loose ball, he lost his sense of direction and ran 65 yards toward the wrong goal. One of his teammates ran him down and tackled him just before he scored for the opposing team. The strange play came in the first half. At half-time, the UCLA players filed off the field and into the dressing room. As others sat down on the benches and the floor, Riegels put a blanket around his shoulders, sat down in a corner, and put his face in his hands.

A football coach usually has a great deal to say to his team during halftime. That day Coach Price was quiet.

When the timekeeper came in and announced that there were three minutes before playing time, Price looked at the team and said, "Men, the same team that played the first half will start the second." The players got up and started out, all but Riegels. He didn't budge. The coach looked back and called to him. Riegels didn't move.

Price went over to where Riegels sat and said, "Roy, didn't you hear me? The same team that played the first half will start the second." Riegels looked up, his cheeks wet with tears.

"Coach," he said," I can't do it. I've ruined you. I've ruined the university's reputation. I've ruined myself. I can't face that crowd out there."

Price reached out, put his hand on Riegel's shoulder and said, "Roy, get up and go on back. The game is only half over." Riegels finally did get up. He went onto the field, and the fans saw him play hard and play well.

THE END

All of us have run a long way in the wrong direction at times. But remember, because of God's mercy, the game is only half over.

"If you, LORD, should mark iniquities, O LORD, who could stand? But there is forgiveness with You, That You may be feared." (Psalm 130:2-4) City Gate Church bulletin, Gallatin, TN.

When things go against you there are three basic choices you have in life:

1. You can rebel and turn back.
2. You resign and walk away.
3. You can rebuild what was destroyed.

If we choose to rebuild, no matter how destructive the challenges of life are, we will be better for it. And don't think rebuilding will be without opposition. Ask Nehemiah who had two hounds on his heels named Sanballat and Tobiah who tried their best to stop him. (Nehemiah 6:1-2)

Another thing, we will be shamed and belittled for the quality of what we are building. Ask Noah! The more you are discouraged by your critics, the more it's an encouraging sign that you are doing the right thing.

If not for hope the heart would break!

This ends the study, but it doesn't end the search for Spiritual truth and meaning to life's challenges. My point is this: God is a God of power and wisdom who can get underneath our problems (rubble) and give us a reason for living (breakthrough) enabling us to rise above the rubble (circumstances) and dance on them. You and God together can form a love compact that Satan cannot penetrate or destroy. Such unity so powerful that it can eradicate fear itself. Fear may be the glue that keeps you stuck, but faith is the solvent that sets you free in the righteous name of Jesus Christ.

Each day pray:

"Lord, guide me to someone today so that I can share your love with them." Because when I see you face-to-face, I cannot bear the thought of coming into your presence and you ask me, "Why did you come alone?"

> "Now unto Him that is able to keep you from falling [stumbling], And to present you faultless before the presence of His glory with exceeding joy. To the all wise God, our Savior, be glory and majesty, dominion and power. Both now and ever." Amen. (Jude 24-25)

THE END

Some Who Have Learned to Dance on the Rubble

I realize that everyone has a story and most believers have a testimony regarding God's active presence in their lives. I have included testimonies of several individuals who I believe are shining examples of how, with their deep faith in God, they worked through their life challenges and have learned how to dance. It is my sincere hope that you will find them inspiring and encouraging so that you, too, will understand is waiting for you: a life filled with joy and freedom.

Keegan Kennedy's Story

Keegan is my great niece; she was born September 9, 1991. Within days of her birth, she showed signs of breathing distress, and stopped breathing at home when she was two weeks old. She was flown to Children's Hospital in Washington D.C. where eventually the doctors found a blood vessel wrapped around her airway which caused extensive damage. Keegan's condition was grave; she suffered respiratory distress and several arrests. She required a tracheotomy and a breathing apparatus called a CPAP to keep her alive. Even with the assistance of these devices, she experienced a full respiratory and cardiac arrest for twenty-four minutes. She was clinically dead for those minutes.

With the help of God, her doctors and nurses, Keegan survived her first two years of life. At that point she was big enough to have her airway reconstructed; the surgery was successful, and Keegan has been able to breathe normally ever since. While Keegan's breathing problem was resolved with reconstructive surgery, the arrests left her with brain damage, and a diagnosis of cerebral palsy. Keegan uses a walker to get around at home and a power wheelchair away from home. Her speech is difficult to understand.

Keegan has an amazing personality and outlook on life. When memories of her illness arise, she responds in her slow speech, "I'm so glad I did not die." She loves life and brings joy to everyone who knows her. She never complains about her disabilities and loves everyone unconditionally.

Among Keegan's life passions is her love of country music. She walks for hours each day with her iPod and headphones singing loudly off key and is happy as can be. Keegan LOVES Blake Shelton, and she has all of Blake's CDs. Jokingly she says she is going to marry him.

Keegan just graduated from Battlefield High School and soon will be twenty years old. Her graduation was unforgettable when she rode across the stage in her wheelchair to receive her diploma. There were 688 graduates in her class, and they gave her a big ovation. To top it off, her sister Sarah who graduated the night before from college was waiting for Keegan at the end of the stage with a big hug.

If you are reading this story about Keegan and feel hopeless about your future, just remember that *"all things work together for good to those who love God and who are called according to His purpose."* (Romans 8:21) and believe that you too can say as Keegan does, "I love my life."

Guess who danced at her high school prom? You guessed it, Keegan did. A young man named Austin invited her to the prom and they danced together. It was amazing! If Keegan can dance on the rubble, you can too!

The Home Going of Matthew Jett (as told by his father Tony Jett)

As I was putting the finishing touches to this book, I received the following story from Tony and Ann Jett via e-mail. Tony and Ann have been friends of ours since the late 1960's. Tony and I attended college together. After college, we went our separate geographical directions to pastor and minister. We basically kept in touch via our mutual friends, but we rarely saw each other.

Recently they came for a rare visit. It was during that visit that Tony shared the story of their son Matthew. Shortly after they returned home, Tony called to tell us how he and Ann enjoyed their visit. It was during that telephone call that Tony shared with me the more personal details of their son Matthew's death and their spiritual struggle both after learning of Matthew's leukemia diagnosis and after his death. When I heard about their struggle with Matt's death and how they coped with their grief, I asked Tony if he and Ann would be willing to share their story in my book. They agreed.

The Jett family has endured much emotional pain and grief in the untimely death of their son Matthew, and no family I know of has shown more courage and faith in their Lord and Savior Jesus Christ than they have. Here is Tony's personal testimony in his own words.

What do you do when you've done all you can do?

What do I do when I have given faithfully all that I can? When I have sacrificed my life for the cause of Christ, served in the ministry, preached the gospel, and have been steadfast all my life, and after all that, God takes the most precious thing in my life from me? As death struck my home, I was totally unprepared for such a thing to happen to a person like me. Broken and discouraged, confused and weakened, I pressed on with a great hurt and emptiness. I lived on in my anguish with feelings of abandonment and betrayal, groping in my darkness to lay hold on what and why God would do such a thing to me. My wandering mind struggled with endless questions of all the thoughts of my unworthiness and what great sin could I have possibly done to make God so angry with me? This answer I could not find.

I was raised in a Pentecostal preacher's home. Our home has always been a home of faith and prayer. I lived all my youth for the Lord, and the Lord saw me through all the troublesome years that most teenagers go through. I married a wonderful young Spirit-filled girl, and in my very early twenties I began to feel the call to the ministry. Married with two very young children, I enrolled in college to prepare myself for whatever God would lead me toward.

At the very beginning of ministry, my passion was in reaching out to the "undesirables." I felt called to go where no one else would go and stay longer than anyone else would stay. I became a church plant-er and, after forty years, I was working on yet another church plant in Franklin, Louisiana. By then we had three children. Our two sons were then young, ordained ministers themselves. Our daughter was a very talented and gifted pianist. Our oldest son Matthew was everything that I wanted to be. He was tall, soft spoken, with the sweetest personality which drew needy people to him. Matt served as our music minister.

Our second son Clint was more like me. Hard working, determined, outgoing, and would usually not backup from anything. While our daughter Christy served as our church pianist, she would drive home from college so that she could minister in every church service or special event that we needed her for. With the great joy of working together, these kids were such an asset to our own ministry.

We were in the final stages of completing a beautiful new three building complex for our new church plant. God had miraculously brought us through every challenge that ministry faces in such a project as this. Then came the news that shattered our lives when the doctors told us that our son Matt had incurable leukemia, and they gave him no more than three years at the outside to live. It felt like someone had literally knocked the wind out of me. Only twenty-six years old with two little children, a little boy of four and a little girl of eight, Matt faced this staggering horror. The joy of our lives, our love and happiness will no longer be with us.

I remember so well, trying to find sleep and could not. I remember walking the house and yard at all hours of the night praying and crying out to God. For two and a half years I would wake up in a frenzy at all hours of the night, and for a split-second wonder if it was a nightmare I was having, only to realize that it was not, and my beautiful son was dying.

I remember rebuking the devil, claiming scriptures, hearing people telling me what to believe. I remember each day smiling and looking into the hollow eyes of my dying son saying, "God is going to heal you." I remember like it was yesterday when Matt would come home from his appointment with the doctor bringing a bad report of his extremely high white blood cell count as the icy grip of fear would again freeze my heart. This horrible indictment of death upon my son's life seemed more than we could bear.

I remember how I continued to work during those final days of the new building program. I remember sobbing so hard that I could not see the nails, pleading for God not to take my son. Not the one that was so good, so innocent and loved so dearly. "God," I cried out in bitterness, "what about the drug dealers, that pedophile, that child abuser, and wife beater? What about the dregs and unproductive liabilities of our society? Why my good son? Why not those who do not deserve to live? God, what about Matt's young wife and little children, who is going to take Matt's place for them?" What about my wife, Matt's mother, who has been so faithful through the years to raise these children who put their faith in you? about all that, God?"

One Sunday night Matt had a terrible headache but did not want to go to the hospital. I sat up with him for a while then went home. I had no idea that this was the beginning of Matt's last few days on earth, or I would have never left his side. Matt's wife called us very early the next morning and said Matt was in such pain that he was willing to go to the hospital, so we rushed him to the hospital in New Orleans. We spent the rest of the day there with Matt. And about 11:00 that night I left to spend the night at Clint's apartment, some thirty miles away, planning to return early in the morning. Early the next morning at about 3:00 A.M. I received a phone call from my wife that the hospital had done a code blue on Matt, and they didn't know if he would make it or not. We rushed back to the hospital only to find out that Matt had gone to be with the Lord. Matt's wife, her father, my wife, younger son and daughter stood around Matt's bedside saying our last good-bye. With just a sheet covering Matt to his chest and the warmth of life beginning to leave his beautiful body, we joined hands, and I began to pray.

My whole prayer was a prayer of thanksgiving. I thanked God for all the wonderful times we had shared together. I thanked God for the talent that He had given Matt and the call of ministry he had placed upon Matt's life. I thanked God that we had successfully seen Matt from his mother's womb to the arms of our Lord. I thanked God for the joy he brought into our lives and for every good thing we have experienced with Matt. In that moment of our unmeasurable grief, and the great tears of pain and loss which filled that hospital room, I ended my prayer with this assurance. I cried out to the Lord with the greatest passion of hurt and faith; I assured our Lord that I didn't know why He was doing this. I cried out, "I don't know; I don't understand, and I don't agree with you that you would do such a thing to us." In our closing moments with Matt's body lying in that hospital bed, I told our Lord, no matter our questions and our pain, through all of this, we are going to trust you and somehow you are going to make it right. We will one day have peace and agree with your plan.

As we left Matt's body at hospital, we set about the task of planning the coming funeral. Through the misery of the moment, we had to plan a memorial service for Matt. I knew that we had to honor our son and speak at the funeral, but in my state of mind, I really had no idea of what I could have good to say about such a great season of loss.

As I prayed for guidance, a very close friend of mine, Dr. Roy H. Cantrell called me from Tennessee to offer his love and support. In his encouragement, Dr. Cantrell shared a scripture with me from Matthew

11:4-6. This, God's Word, answered every question I was struggling with. I knew that this was a sure word straight from the heart of our God. Dr. Cantrell reminded me of the words of Jesus when John the Baptist, the great forerunner of Christ, had his own confidence shaken in our Lord. Jesus sent back word to John saying: "Go and show John again those things which you hear and see: The blind receives their sight and the lame walk, the lepers are cleansed and the deaf hear, the dead are raised up, and the poor have the gospel preached to them. And blessed is he who is not offended in me."

After the funeral, with a weakened but determined spirit, we moved ahead recovering a day at a time, while the healing process of our Lord began to mend us. It surely wasn't over in one night, but through many days, months, and years, the Lord has been faithful. They say that one of the credentials of a successful minister is that his children serve the Lord. Well, by that measure, I am successful today. I have a son who is in the presence of the Lord, a son working on his doctorate, and a daughter who is still ministering in music.

If we could see the future, we would see that the Lord always take care of our future, no matter what today may hold. Today, Matt's wife Theresa is married to a fine young minister, and they are serving a great church in Louisiana. Matt's son Dustin is today an ordained Pentecostal minister who serves full time as a music minister in a great church in Oklahoma. Matt's daughter Bethany is now married to a fine young Christian man, and they are missionaries winning the lost to Jesus. And by the way, we have another generation of ministers in Matt's family that God is raising up for His service. Young Ethan, our great-grandson and Matt's grandchild, has already preached his first sermon at the age of eight.

Isn't the Lord faithful? The Scriptures always come alive when we are faithful. And again, we are reminded in Romans 8:35-37: "Who shall separate us from the love of Christ? Shall tribulation, or distress, or persecution, or famine or nakedness, or peril of sword (or death)? No in all these things we are more than conquerors through Him that loved us." Am I still angry with God? Absolutely not! Do I understand yet what God allowed? I do not!

Do I still trust Him? He is sweeter now than he has ever been to me. One day we will see Jesus and Matt. Could it be possible that our father has allowed me to share with him in the sacrifice of the death of His own Son? Heaven will revel great and many profound truths.

Injured by Matt's death, and through intense pain we were brought into greater fellowship with God. To God be the glory! Amen!

> Some of the most forgiving people are those who have gone through the worst trials imaginable.

Samuel Said's Story
I was born in Nazareth in the hills of Galilee and raised in the village of Josephus (KfarYasif). I am Arab.

I refer to Our Lord as my neighbor. The thought that remains with me is this: what do I do and how do I live when my next-door neighbor is the Creator of the universe? I walked where he walked; I breathed the same air he breathed; I ate the same kind of food he ate; I walked the same land; I drank the water He walked upon, and I played hide and seek around His house.

At a very young age, the Lord saved me and called me to be a part of His ministry abroad to the English-speaking people. I attended church every single night as we lived above the church building; every night I would attend Bible study and prayer meeting where I witnessed to Arabs and Jews who were supposed to hate one another and shared the love of Christ in a holy manner. God's call was so overwhelming that I started preaching God's word at the age of fourteen.

When I was eighteen, I left my country seeking theological training to equip myself for a ministry. In 1985, I graduated from Elim Bible College in the United Kingdom (UK), was ordained as a Baptist minister and set apart to serve God abroad. I spent most of my life in the UK and the USA preaching in many different churches: Arabic, Messianic Jewish, and English-speaking.

In 1988, I experienced a head injury which caused 85% memory loss, a back injury that left me bedridden for two years, resulting in being categorized disabled for twelve years. Every part of my being was tested; my faith was tested in every way. The only thing that I was able to trust was God's Word. The doctors would administer drugs three times a day, so I decided to listen to the Word of God for two hours, three times a day. After one year and no significant recovery, I came to the point of giving up on life. I asked the Lord: "Why don't You heal me?" His answer was evident every time. "I healed you 2,000 years ago; get up and walk." My response was always the same, "I can't get up; heal me, please." One night I asked Him to heal me or take me to heaven. His answer was so compelling that it shocked me. He said, "Do you believe your symptoms or my Word?"

That very night when He called me by name, the pain left my back, and I got up! His Word says, ". . . He was wounded for our transgressions, He was bruised for our iniquities; the chastisement for our peace was upon Him, and by His stripes, we are healed." (Isiah 53:5) It also says, "I can do all things through Christ who strengthens me." (Philippians 4:13) Though I had my physical and spiritual challenges, I did not allow them to stop me living for the Lord. The Lord healed my back, but I continued to suffer from migraine headaches 24/7 until July 2011 when the Lord visited me in a dream and healed me from the migraines.

The Lord Jesus taught me a great lesson. I should not allow my circumstances to change or control me. Because of Christ who is in me, I have the power to change my circumstances to keep in the will of God. I cannot stop circumstances from coming my way. What I do with them will change the direction of my life. His Word also says that we should cast all of our cares upon Him because He cares for us. (2 Peter 5:7).

I trust in the Word of God as I seek Jesus daily through the power of the Holy Spirit, and I find him. (Jeremiah 29:12-14) I have stopped asking the Lord to bless me because His Word tells me in Ephesians 1:3 that I have been blessed with every heavenly blessing. So, I trust Him, love Him, obey Him, follow him to grow in His likeness.

Novella Brewer's Story

My sister Novella is an adult now, but when she was very young, she was afflicted with polio. This is her story as told to me. She can vaguely remember the hospital stay in Milton, West Virginia, and she remembers nothing about being in an iron lung. She only remembers walking down a path with some nurses to where several other medical people were looking at her through a black iron fence. Her memory is that the iron bars made her feel caged like an animal.

When she started school, there were questions in her mind about why she was crippled, unlike the other kids. One day she asked Mother why she got polio and why none of the other children had gotten it. She recalls that Mother posed a question to her. She said, "Novella, if you could give your crippled arm to one of your siblings right now, which one would you give it to?" Her answer was, "I wouldn't give it to either one of them because they couldn't stand it." Her answer revealed the pain that she had gone through. She didn't wish it visited on anyone else in the family.

Her crippled arm has certainly affected her life. She told me about the time she wanted to mop the floor when she was a little girl, and Mother told her that she couldn't do it because she was unable to wring the mop dry enough with one hand. She kept pleading with Mother to let her mop the floor. While the debate was going on between them, Dad had been listening. He came to Novella's aid and said, "Let her try it; if she can't wring out the mop, you can dry the floor later." Novella put the mop handle between her legs, wrapped her ankles around it, and squeezed the water out of the mop with one hand. She did an admirable job of mopping and drying the floor that day, and that gave her the confidence to face other challenges.

In her teen years, she was given the opportunity to go to Chicago to have surgery on her dislocated shoulder. The doctors wanted to fuse her arm to her shoulder which would result in giving her more mobility and strength to do things. All during her growing up years, Novella questioned why everyone in her entire community was polio free except for her. Then she went to Chicago for surgery. She explained to me that the event was like what Oprah Winfrey calls a "light bulb moment." Novella's "light bulb" came on when she was admitted to the hospital along with twenty-seven other young people who needed some type of corrective surgery. She noticed that all of them were in wheelchairs. Not one of them could walk.

When she saw how blessed she was to be able to walk, she ran errands for the other patients—mostly carrying food and drinks to them. It was then that she thanked God for answering Mother's prayers. [Mother had prayed for God to spare Novella from being unable to walk.] It was then that she began to appreciate her ability to walk. She stopped feeling sorry for herself for having a paralyzed arm. Her experience was much like the man who said, "I complained that I had no shoes until I saw a man who had no feet." Another "light bulb" moment for her came when she went back to the doctor after the surgery for a follow up visit. The doctor told her that of his six hundred polio patients, she was the only one who did not have a curved spine. His news verified that her ability to walk was an answer to prayer.

When asked if she sees any "blessings" in being physically challenged, she replied: "They are too numerous to tell." She went on to say that the thing that appeared to be her weakness had become her strength because one is only crippled if they think they are. The fact that she can walk is always a reminder of God's mercy to her. Of course, she has wondered what it would it be like to toss a child into the air with both arms or reach up into the cabinet with one hand and take down a dish. But those things she can't do pale in comparison to what she can do. She concluded our discussion by saying, "And, furthermore, I believe my experience has changed my life. It has drawn me closer to God."

Three years ago, she ended her thirty-five-year journey teaching Sunday School at her church in Lorain, Ohio. She has seen many of the children called into several ministries. One, in particular, became the youth leader of the church and is presently the pastor of a church in New York. Twenty years ago (while still teaching), she began working in an assisted living facility where she is presently working. God not only fulfilled her calling to teach; He has also given her countless opportunities to lead many of the elderly to the saving knowledge of Jesus Christ. Many were church attenders, yet they had never heard of being "born again."

She is nearing 70 years old and stands in awe of the journey on which God has taken her thus far. She excitedly anticipates the next twenty or so years should God allow her journey to continue. To God be all the glory, honor and praise!

Because of a praying mother and a brother who yielded to the call of God to preach the gospel (and never give up) she is saved today! Novella says, "Never stop praying, It moves the hand of God."

Jeff Henley's Story
I've been a Christian for most of my adult life, being baptized around the age of twelve. My family was never really church goers, but both of my grandmothers were, and they always wanted to share their faith

with me. They always referred to me as a miracle child due to the fact that when I was a nine-month-old infant, I had fallen out of my father's truck camper onto the Dan Ryan expressway in downtown Chicago during rush hour. My family was asleep in the back while I crawled around, and out I went. An Army soldier, just home from Vietnam, and his wife and child saw what they thought was a baby doll and stopped to pick me up out of live traffic. Well the next thing you know there I was on the cover of the *Chicago Tribune*! That's another story for another day, but that day proved God had his mighty hand on me!

Fast forward fifty-two years to February 10, 2016, to the Sumner County diagnostic clinic. I had gone in for a routine upper GI test due to some issues swallowing. Dr. Robert Uhle came out and in his matter of fact manner informed me that I had esophageal cancer and from the size of the tumor in my esophagus it was in an advanced stage.

The only words I can use next to begin to describe my emotions Is complete and utter devastation. My wife and I were in a complete death spiral, and I truly uttered these words: "I wonder what God wants me to do with this." Within minutes we reached out to our children and family members. I had to go home. I needed time to catch my breath, but unbeknownst to me, my son had run into an old friend whom we hadn't seen in a couple of months and he told him about the diagnosis. Well, that friend was Howie Cantrell; he prayed with me and my wife and invited us to church. We took him up on that offer. It was there that my wife and I learned again to pray, and specifically it's where our prayers formed. My prayer was as follows: "Dear Heavenly Father, please hold this cancer in your hand and do not let it spread to any other parts of my body." During my radiation treatments my wife added ". . . and when they open him up to remove the cancer, let it be dead where it lays."

Cancer is not pretty; it's one of the hardest things we can fight against here on earth. My treatments were hard, and over a period of thirty-five days I received radiation daily and chemotherapy every Wednesday for eight weeks. To say that I was exhausted and sick is an understatement, but church members and small group support kept up our spirits. Our church prayed over me several times, but one night in particular Howie called me up and the group laid hands on me. I felt it like I had been hit by a hammer; something in my body changed. I knew it right away. Our daily prayer never wavered; morning, noon, and night my wife and I prayed.

On June 13th, I was admitted to the Centennial Medical Center (the Sarah Cannon Cancer Center) and at 8:30 a.m. I was taken back for my surgery. This particular kind of surgery is very brutal. One patient in thirty dies on the table. So, Howie anointed me, and we prayed as a family in the little room in which I was waiting, and I found it odd that I wasn't even nervous. I was oddly very calm about what was coming. I remember looking at my wife as they were wheeling me out and thinking how blessed I truly was, for everything the Lord had provided me.

Through the fog of anesthesia in the recovery room I remember talking with my daughter and son, unsure if it was real or a dream. My next memory is firm; a gruff nurse was telling me that I was almost ready to rest, all I needed to do was move from the rolling bed to my bed in the room. I've never heard so many people gasp at one time, for I stood up, turned around, and sat back down. This action is a testament in itself for it was the power of God Almighty who moved me!

Hours and days passed; I could not eat or drink until the following Monday (seven days later). I walked each day, prayed all day, and through it all my wife never left my side. She prayed over me all day and night as I was still highly medicated and slept most of my days. Finally the day came for my test, a leak test for what remained of my esophagus, I passed! That day was full of surprises, the first being my pathology report from my stomach surgeon, This is the moment we had been waiting for, then these words came out the doctor's mouth: "Mr. Henley, your pathology report came back with great news. There is no sign of cancer in your body; we even lifted 20 additional lymph nodes. It was as though someone had their hand wrapped around your tumor. It did not spread anywhere!"Tears of joy, excitement, and absolute wonder filled us as the Lord confirmed He had answered prayer when the doctor had used the exact words! I love it when our Heavenly Father shows off! A further confirmation came a little later in the day when my other surgeon came to see me. She was responsible for my lung. It had to be collapsed and removed during surgery for others to have room to put me back together. She also shared pathology reports with us and, lo and behold, after telling us there was no cancer, she said all that remained of the tumor was a blob-like mass, dead where it laid! Hearing our exact prayer words from the doctor we knew it was God's hand at work.

This all happened over three and a half years ago, I am still cancer free through the Grace of God! I share this story with everyone I can. Just retelling it again here makes me feel amazing! To this day, I know that my Father has something more for me. I attend church faithfully, and God speaks with me as a father would to his son. He called me to tithe, so I tithe; he called me to step up to become an able Elder in His church and I accepted! I don't know what God's plans are for me, but I do know when He calls, I will answer and follow.

The Simple ABC's of Salvation

A   **Admit** that you are a sinner. (Romans 3:23)

B   **Believe** that Jesus died and arose from the grave to purchase you a place in heaven that He offers as a free gift. (Romans 6:23 and Ephesians 2:8,9)

C   **Confess** your sins to Christ who is "faithful and just to forgive us ours and to cleanse us from all unrighteousness." (1 John 1:9)

Pray This Prayer

Jesus, I admit that I am a sinner. I believe that you died on the cross to purchase me a place in heaven that you offer as a free gift. I confess that I have sinned against You, and that I am not worthy of this gift. You promised in Revelation 3:20 that if I would open the door to my heart, confess my sins, and invite You into my heart, You would make me a part of your family. In Jesus' name, I open my heart and invite You to come in; I ask for forgiveness of my sins, and I transfer my faith from my good works and myself to you alone for my salvation. I receive you as the resurrected and living Christ and as my Lord and Savior. Amen.

My Commitment

Now that I have received the gift of eternal life and know that I am your child, I commit my life to you **to do all that you command me to do**.

I further commit to . . .
>   **Praying** to establish a closer relationship with You.
>   **Studying** the Bible to grow in Your Word and wisdom.
>   **Sharing** my testimony with others.
>   **Fellowshipping** with other believers (Hebrews 10:25).
>   **Worshipping** to praise you and glorify Your Name.

Poems From and For the Soul

Don't Meddle with God
Roy H. Cantrell

You can meddle with the devil,
but don't meddle with God.
Don't meddle with His Church,
or even with the synagogue.

You can meddle with the devil,
but don't meddle with the Word.
Because your perversion and
Aversion to His version is absurd.

You can meddle with the devil,
but don't meddle with God's plan.
Salvation is by grace through faith.
Anything less is building on sand.

You can meddle with the devil,
but don't meddle with God's leaders.
If you do touch His anointed ones,
you won't get to be a repeater.

You can meddle with the devil
To your little heart's desire.
But don't you meddle with God's stuff
unless you have plans to expire.

The First

Roy H. Cantrell

Jesus,
I can only imagine the angelic hosts'
anticipation of your birth and them
peering over Heaven's balcony to
witness your first breath of pure air
that would bring joy to the world
and salvation to all who believe.

Jesus,
I can only imagine your first smile as
infant God-man, Creator of all things,
and heaven's resounding applause.
The stars communicating in sync,
your birth in heaven's starlit code from
galaxy to galaxy in twinkles and winks.

Jesus,
I can only imagine the first time Mary
held you close to her breast and
counted your fingers and toes in
admiration of your God-like perfection.
In wonderment recalling your.
Immaculate conception. God Incarnate!

Jesus,
I can only imagine your first laugh,
and the sound echoing through the universe.
The angelic host joining in with Holy! Holy! Holy!
All creation coming alive and laughing with you.
The flowers smiling back in multiple floral colors,
and all living creatures bow in silence at the
declaration: God lives!

Jesus,
I can only imagine your moments of merriment
when you turned the water into wine, witnessed
to the woman at the well, raised Lazarus from the dead,
rescued the woman in adultery from death, and healed
the woman with the issue of blood, restored
Peter to ministry and defeated Satan even in death.
Knowing that we are saved by your amazing grace,
and how Satan hates laughter, but how you love it.
Grant us the joy and life of holy laughter.
In your name we pray!
Amen.

Joy
Roy H. Cantrell

Joy is the water in a well
That a bucket pulls up
When you are thirsty.

Joy is the strength
That enters your soul
When you are weak.

Joy is a song
That comes in the night
When you're discouraged.

Joy is the oil
That soothes the soul
When life is the roughest.

Joy is a word
That lifts the spirit
When everything is silent.

Joy is food
That feeds the inner man
When he is famished.

Joy is assurance
That breeds faith
When unbelief abounds.

Joy is praise
On the lips
When others are mute.

Joy is a sound
That always lifts you
When you are down.

Joy in a home
Can hold it together
When it is falling apart.

Exceeding joy
Is knowing God loves you
No matter what.

Love Lasts Forever
Roy H. Cantrell

"I love you," is said to people,
and even to dogs and cats,
to God, to the sun and moon,
to cars, houses, and even rats.

"I love you," is said to companies,
to pillows and a comfortable bed,
to money, to the stock market,
and even to those who are dead.

"I love you," is said to one and all. To
anything that moves, sits, or crawls,
to movies, games, Facebook friends,
to those we don't even know at all.

"I love you," ought to be used carefully
because love is a sacred word you see.
It's the only things you can take to heaven
with you. If in heaven you plan to be.

So, use "love" as often as you wish,
Just be sure when you say it
that you mean what you say,
and what you say is not amiss.

Nothing
Roy H. Cantrell

Nothing means no thing, no exceptions!
That's what it's supposed to mean, you see.
Why do we say nothing means no thing,
then define nothing as we please?

Nothing but grace and faith saves us;
we shout to high heaven that it's true.
Yet, we work from daylight to dark,
to make sure we follow all the rules.

Nothing can snatch us out of God's hand.
We declare we're safe there forever more.
Yet in the very next breath, we worry that
God's grip is weaker than thought before.

Nothing can separate us from God's love.
We pen songs and sing them in gratitude.
Then, when we make a stupid mistake,
we're no longer sure that His love is true.

We believe God can keep us from falling.
Our coins declare that it's all about trust.
Yet our actions do not back it up,
So we build safety nets to catch us.

Only God can present us faultless.
This is just an out-and-out fact.
But no one is perfect in this world,
so our perfection is only an act.

Now, with all these facts presented.
Does nothing really mean nothing?
The dictionary says it does, but we say,
"No, not unless we first define the thing."

If nothing doesn't mean no thing,
We're lying to ourselves, that's true.
Because Jesus paid for it all on the cross,
there's absolutely nothing more we can do.

Be Still

Roy H. Cantrell

"Be still" are the two words that I remember most when growing up. My earliest memory of hearing them was when dad cut my hair. He was not a professional barber but did a decent job. He used hand clippers that occasionally pulled my hair instead of cutting it. This resulted in me shrugging my shoulders much like a turtle pulling its head inside its shell. I was already fidgety from the heat, sweat, and hair down my shirt that Hindered dad's progress and resulted in his "be still" plea for the zillionth time.

"Be still" means more to me know that I'm grown than it did when dad said it to try to keep me still to cut my hair when I was a child. Our heavenly Father wants our attention so that He can minister to our needs, but he can't do it unless we stop paying less attention to what is going on in the world and spend more time with Him. There is a verse in the Bible that says, "Be still and know that I am God." (Psalm 46: 10-11) To "be still" is to listen and pay attention. To "be still" is never to fully know God and never To receive His full benefits for our lives.

Great Peace
Roy H. Cantrell

Great Peace, that reigns sublime.
A heavenly peace, harmony of the soul.
A gentle rhythm of the Holy Spirit,
a beat that says all is under control.

Great Peace, that shouts "victory!"
and assures you that, "all is well."
Even during your worst trial and
assault from the abyss of hell.

Great Peace, is a newborn
Cuddled in his mother's arms.
Oblivious to the world's terror,
showing no fear or alarm.

Great Peace, is a calm and trust
that earthly words can't describe.
It can only be known in knowing.
The Prince of Peace, Jesus Christ!

But God

Roy H. Cantrell

Remember when your
loved one died, and
you were left alone?
But God!

Remember when you
lost your job, and
you were homeless?
But God!

Remember when you
were lied about, and
your reputation was in tatters?
But God!

Remember when your
doctor said there was
no cure for your disease?
But God!

Remember when there
seemed to be no hope
for that prodigal child?
But God!

Remember when you
strayed from God,
and you saw no way back?
But God!

Remember when your
companion walked out on you
and your life was awful?
But God!

Remember when you
cried out to God, and
He delivered you
out of it all?
But God!

Praise Him! Amen!

Look Out!

Roy H. Cantrell

Look out for the Devil;
he is a trickster, for sure.
Whatever he does or
says is never pure.

There are two major tricks
that he pulls out of his hat.
He deceives millions daily,
and that is a matter of fact.

His first slight-of-hand is
to discourage the heart.
He makes you believe that
you are a useless part.

His second slight-of-hand is
to make you doubt.
Just like discouragement
it comes the same route.

So, look out for Satan, and
his two magic tricks.
Think: to work his magic
he knows who to pick.

Then how do you stop
such a deceiver as he?
Claim the blood of Jesus,
and watch the trickster flee.

Keep Looking Up
Roy H. Cantrell

The Emmaus Road
we all must trod
with a broken heart,
head bowed to God.

The news is bad,
our hearts are sad.
Jesus is dead, and
the world is glad.

A stranger appears
with a hearty smile.
He said, "Look up,
trust me in this trial."

"Join me for a meal, and
your hurts will be healed."
Suddenly He was gone.
It was my Jesus, for real.

Life is truly a struggle
that's a birthing fact.
You arrived in the world
with a push and a smack.

Your journey began
the day you were born.
On the Emmaus Road
you'll go, heart torn.
"So, keep looing up,"
and Me you will see.
"One day you will be
as Me, struggle free!"

Prayer

Roy H. Cantrell

Prayer is:
a sin killer,
a life giver,
a door opener,
a vision seeker,
a power supplier,
a victory maker,
a saint producer,
a problem solver,
a stain remover,
a Jesus revealer.
Infinity!

So, Pray!

Making a Daily Devotion Plan

Make a Daily Devotion Plan

You can't really have a sustainable devotional plan without some rules or guidelines. Don't panic when I mention rules. I'm not a big fan of a lot of rules, especially religious ones. Sometimes, however, they are necessary to support and enable spiritual growth in one's life.

The word for rule comes from the Greek language. It's the word trellis. Does that surprise you? A trellis serves as a tool that enables vines to climb. The trellis makes it possible for a grape vine to climb up it so that the vine can produce more grapes. It can serve as a side garden for squash, beans, tomatoes, and other vine-growing fruits and vegetables.

Trellises [rules of life] are meant to aid us to be more fruitful, spiritually speaking, and to make us more productive Christians. Rules should serve the purpose to draw us closer to God and not just be one more task to perform. See the poem entitled "Rules" in the poetry appendix.

We may unconsciously be following guidelines but have never written them down. Take time to make a list of what you are doing in your devotion. Remember, no one's rules are exactly the same. Be careful not to get into a rut. A rut is a grave with both ends knocked out. To guard against a devotion becoming stagnant, we might want to change things around and do them differently occasionally. Please remember to tailor your devotional plan to what is best and right for you.

Devotion Suggestions

Here are some ideas you may want to consider helping you put together a devotion plan, or if you already have one, you might find one or two ideas to add to yours.

- Select a quiet place where you are not interrupted. If you don't have one, think about getting up early while everyone is asleep.
- Music can be a real blessing. More and more people are downloading music on their iPhones and listening with headsets while they have their devotion.
- You may want to begin with the Lord's Prayer [it's really "our"

prayer]. Some people learn to pray The Lord's Prayer in Spanish or some language other than their own. They also learn Bible verses in another language. I memorized Isaiah 53:5 in Hebrew. That's just me.

- "Bless His name." You can use Dr. Larry Lea's *Prayer Guide* that lists the names of Jehovah and what those names mean. Personalize the significance of the name and its appropriate meaning; for example: Jehovah Shalom "God is our Peace." Pray for peace over you and your family, our nation, and others.

- Quote your favorite verse(s) that come to mind. I might only quote one of these several times. I raise my hands and declare, "I am the righteousness of God by His mercy and grace." Usually I quote Ephesians 2:8-9 and Jude 24-25 and some of Romans, Chapter 8, along with Isaiah 53:5 and Jeremiah 30:17. I write a lot, and with Parkinson's, I'm finding it more difficult to type. Before I begin writing, I quote psalm 144:1, "Blessed be the Lord my Rock, who trains my hands for war, and my fingers for battle." I have a small bottle of oil that I use to anoint myself on the forehead, and I ask God to heal the Parkinson's so that I can think and write. If I am having pain elsewhere, I ask God to heal that pain, too.

- I pray for my wife Kaye and, our two children and their families, the great-grands, and the great- great-grands, as well as those whom the Holy Spirit brings to my mind.

- Remember, the Holy Spirit: "He makes intercession for the saints according to the will of God." Read Romans 8:26-27.

- Some people prefer not to eat anything before they pray. Others enjoy some type of refreshments. Either way, don't fall into Satan's trap of condemnation if you occasionally fall short of keeping "the rules."

- If you miss your quiet time, pray a silent prayer as you go about your daily duties. If you have a hard time falling asleep at night, quote Bible verses for peace of mind.

- Please don't compare your guidelines with others. Everyone needs a relationship with the Heavenly Father, and each is different, just as everyone's retina, ear, or fingerprint DNA are different.

- Be yourself. God loves your uniqueness. You are who you are on purpose. You were born with a purpose. Your job is to discover what that purpose is.
- Recently, James Seals, Pastor of Mount Olive Ministries, Cleveland, Tennessee, was speaking about his personal time with God. He said, "When I open my Bible, the Author of the book [God] shows up." That is the truth. He also said that he had over 40 Christian songs on his iPhone that he listens to. If you want more of God spend more time with him. "Draw near to God and He will draw near to you. (James 4:8) "Then you will call upon me and go and pray unto me, and I will listen to you." (Jeremiah 29:12)
- If this is your first devotional plan, start with one or two simple rules. Don't feel that God will be mad and punish you if you don't memorize lots of verses or if you forget to pray. Nehemiah prayed an eight-word prayer that brought major results. He said, "So, I prayed to the God of heaven." (Nehemiah 2:4b) However, he certainly prayed more than the eight recorded words, and he surely prayed a lot before he appeared before the king with a sad countenance. His life depended upon it.

A friend of ours, Bishop Wayne Thorne, developed a simple, but powerful, prayer outline that he uses in his devotion. He gave me permission to share it with you. He loves the number seven, so the outline has seven areas that he uses as a guide to pray for seven basic needs.

His outline is as follows:
He prays: "O Lord. Bless me. . ."

- Spiritually
- Physically
- Financially
- Mentally
- With Wisdom
- With fear [awe] of the Lord
- With Increased faith

Bishop Thorn uses these seven steps only as a guide. He told me that he pauses at each step of the outline and waits for the Holy Spirit to impress on him what and for whom to pray.

The Book of Psalms was the songbook or book of praise for the Jewish people. Find a Psalm and just say or sing it out loud in your prayer time. I've found that when I do that, it is like priming a pump. I begin to add my own words of praise to God. Praise invites the Holy Spirit, and rivers and streams of praise begin to pour out of our spirit. Jesus referred to this in John 7:37-38: "On the last day, that great day of the feast [Pentecost], Jesus stood and cried out saying, 'If anyone thirst, let him come to Me and drink. He who believes in Me, as the Scripture has said, out of his belly [heart] will flow rivers of living waters.' "

Jesus was all about life. He said, "The thief does not come except to steal, and to kill, and to destroy. I have come that you may have life, and that you may have it more abundantly." (John 10:10) Think on this: "life more abundantly." The Greek word, *perissos* [per-is-soss] Strong's #4053: "Superabundance, excessive, overflowing, surplus, over and above, more than enough, profuse, more than sufficient." Satan is always trying to convince us that Jesus will not remain with us when the going gets tough. That's Satan's way of discouraging us. But consider this; if you give your very best to God, He will give His very best to you. That is what God did when He gave Himself for us in the person of His Son, Jesus. Satan, on the other hand, came to "steal, kill, and destroy." If you serve Satan that is what you get, but if you live totally for God and His Kingdom, abundant life is what you get.

And whatever you ask in prayer, you will receive, it you have faith.
Matthew 21:22

Prayer Log and Memorial

The intent of this section is to assist you in organizing your prayer requests and logging the effects of your prayers. This section will also serve as a memorial for coming generations who will be blessed by them and give God the praise.

"...Your prayers and your alms have gone up for a memorial before God."
Acts 10:4

Date	Prayer Subject	Answered?	Date

"There is no obstacle too great, no challenge too difficult, if you have faith." Gordon B. Hinkley

"In my distress I cried to the LORD, and He heard me." Psalm 120:1

Date	Prayer Subject	Answered?	Date

"Because He bends down to listen, I will pray as long as I have breath." Psalm 116:2

Spiritual Growth Assessment

God loves us, and since we believe that, we should want to strengthen our spiritual lives so that we can have a better relationship with God and others.

To assist you in this spiritual journey the **spiritual growth assessment** below has been prepared to assist you in identifying your strengths and weaknesses.

Circle one number in each statement below that best represents your answer of how well the statement describes you, or of how frequently you do the activity. Add up the seven numbers to get your final score.

As you have already discovered, there is also a survey numbered 1-7 at the end of each study guide that will help you get a general idea whether you are basically involved in spiritual activity or not.

1) Living
My choices, actions and lifestyle match my beliefs and values. They are in alignment with God's Word.

1   2   3   4   5   6   7   8   9   10

This doesn't describe me. This describes me somewhat. This describes me well

2) Loving
I focus on being a loving person—respecting people and loving God and others.

1   2   3   4   5   6   7   8   9   10

This doesn't describe me This describes me somewhat This describes me well

3) Laughing
When I look back on my life--I didn't laugh a lot.

1   2   3   4   5   6   7   8   9   10

This doesn't describe me. This describes me somewhat. This describes me well

4) Listening
I have a deep desire to communicate with God and Him with me

1   2   3   4   5   6   7   8   9   10

This doesn't describe me. This describes me somewhat This describes me well

5) Learning
In order to have a continued personal spiritual growth, I spend time reading and studying the Bible.

1   2   3   4   5   6   7   8   9   10

This doesn't describe me. This describes me somewhat. This describes me well

6) Leaning
When life is challenging or confusing, I turn to God's Word for comfort and encouragement.

1   2   3   4   5   6   7   8   9   10

This doesn't describe me. This describes me somewhat. This describes me well

7) Letting Go

Rather than simply adopting the beliefs and traditions of others, I have thoughtfully come to my own conclusions. I have an understanding of the life and ministry of Jesus Christ as my Savior and Redeemer and have made my own personal decision to accept Him the as Lord of my life.

1   2   3   4   5   6   7   8   9   10

This doesn't describe me. This describes me somewhat. This describes me well

Your Score is ☐

References

1. Joni Eareckson Tada. https:// www.goodreads.com.

2. "Drug Overdose." STATCAST. September 9, 2019. https://www.cdc. gov.

3. Carl Frederick Buechner. www.frederickbuechner.com/ quote-of-the- day/2017/1/11/yourownjourney.

4. Peter and Geri Scazzero. *Emotionally Healthy Spirituality.* (Grand Rapids: Baker Books, 2005).

5. Hansel, Tim. You *Gotta' Keep Dancin'*, pp. 94-95.

6. Ron Sider. *Emotionally Healthy Spirituality.* "The Scandal of the Evangelical Conference: Why Are Christians Living Just Like the Rest of the World." (Grand Rapids: Baker Books, 2005) p. 13.

7. Hughes, Lawanna. *Freedom Is a Choice.* Copyright 2014, Lawanna N. Hughes, p. 8.

8. Recovery Through Christ is a community program available in several cities. The program in the Middle Tennessee area is co-sponsored by Dr. Howie Cantrell (City Gate Institute, Gallatin, TN) and Dr, Mark Grubbs. Contact the founder Jamie Harper at Jamie Harper/Support at www,recoverythroughchrist.org in Mount Juliet, TN or htpps://faceboook.com>places>Mount Juliet>medical & health.

9. *Psychology Today*.com/us/basis/fear.

10. Viktor E. Frankl and Harold S. Kushner. *Man's Search for Meaning,* 1946.

11. Rick Warren. *The Purpose Driven Life: What Am I Here For?"*

12. "Life," Dr. Roy H. Cantrell.

13. Sister Helen Kelly. www.madtangy. com.>guides-authors>sister-helen-kelly.

14. Richard Arvin Overton. www.cnbc.com.2018.

15. Adrian Rogers. www.oneplace.com>ministries>love-worth-finding. org.

16. James Montgomery Boice. www.oneplace. com>ministries>the-bible-study-hour.

17. Sydney Carter, © 1963 Galliard ltd. Used by permission of Galaxy Music Corporation, NY. Sole U.S. agent. All rights reserved.

18. Dr. Fuchsia Pickett. www.god'swordtowomen.org>healing-pickett.

19. D. L. Moody.www.azquotes.com>author>10304-dwight_l_moody.

20. https://lproof.org

21. Stanley M. Horton. *Tongues and Prophecy.* Gospel Publishing House. Springfield, Missouri.

22. David Alsobrook, *Learning to Love.* Sure Word Ministries.

23. W.A. Criswell. www.wacriswell.com>sermons.

24. Nik Ripkin, *The Insanity of God: The Story of Faith Resurrected.* 2013.

25. Harvard Study on Friendship. Harvard Health Publishing. September 23, 1917.

26. Larry Crabb. *Inside Out.* www.goodreads.com/author/quotes.

27. Dr. D. James Kennedy. Evangelism Explosion.

28. Lewis B. Smedes. *How Can It Be All Right When Everything Is all Wrong?"* 1982.

29. *Spirit Filled Life Bible.* Notation at the bottom of pp. 1699-1700.

30. *Universal Laws Never Before Revealed: Keely's Secrets.* www.ama-zon.com/John Keely.

31. *Spirit Filled Life Bible.* Notation at the bottom of p. 357.

32. Eggleston, Margaret White. *The Use of the Story in Religious Education.* 1920.

33. Helen Keller, quoted in the supplement to her book, *The Story of My Life.* 1903.

34. Ravi Zacharias. www.goodreads.com>author>3577>Ravi_Zacharias.

35. Soren Kierkegaard en.wikipedia.org>wiki>leap_of_faith.

36. Malala Yousafai. www.goodreads.com>author>quotes>7064545. Malala_Yousafai.

37. Merle Shain. www.quotetab.com>quotes>by-merle-shain.

38. Paul Claudel. www.azquotes.com>author>21328-Paul_Claudel.

39. Carl Jung. www.goodreads. com>work>quotes>1621452-antwort-auf-hiob.

40. Jonathan Cahn. *The Oracle; The Jubilean Mysteries Unveiled.* Frontline: Lake Mary, FL. 2019, p. 273.

Suggestions for the Group Leader

The goal of the Study Guide is to help you apply the seven Biblical truths found in *Dancing on the Rubble*.

Here's how to use the Study Guide. The Study Guide has seven chapters containing seven topics that coincide with the text. The Study Guide is designed as both an individual study or a small group study over a seven-week period.

The goal of this seven-week study is to help you take a fresh look at these Biblical truths practiced by flesh and blood people, found both in the Old and New Testament. This study does just that in 7 practical ways.

If you are doing a group study, here are some suggestions to assist you in planning your meetings: please refrain from giving advice—don't do it! Faith-based counselors are advised of the possible illegality of handing out advice if you are not a certified, qualified, licensed counselor. You may discuss choices, and they choose, but don't advise.

1. Briefly share your name and something about yourself; such as what you enjoy doing: (e.g., reading, writing, sports, music, etc.)
2. Briefly explain the seven parts of each lesson.
3. Remember, do not pressure anyone to share.

Prepare for each session.
- Read the chapter in *Dancing on the rubble* that correspond with each session.
- Use the pronoun "I" when sharing.
- Don't preach. Keep your remarks short.
- Let the Holy Spirit lead. Don't try to fix everyone's problems
- Don't think you have to reference every one's comments.
- Confidentiality is seriously important.
- Don't pressure others to share.
- Feel free to share your spiritual walk.
- Be punctual
- When closing, be brief!

Stop...Look...Listen!

It's okay to occasionally "stop" and reflect. There will be "silence in heaven for half- an- hour," someday. "Look" around, observe the mood of the group and "listen" closely to what each person says. What happens in the group, stays in the group.

Suggestion: Accentuate the positive and omit the in-between-stuff.

The group must be a "safe place" for individuals to open-up and share whatever is on their hearts. In order to create such an environment, shared details should not be repeated outside the group.

Suggested Readings

1. *The Paradigm*, Jonathan Cahn, Copyright 2017, www.charisma-house.com
2. *Mysteries*, Jonathan Cahn, Copyright 2016, www.charismahouse.com
3. *The MYSTERY of the SHEMITAH*, Jonathan Cahn, Copyright 2014, www.charismahouse.com
4. *Is This the End?* David Jeremiah, Copyright 1996,2004,2007,2013. Yates &Yate, LLP.www.yate2.com
5. *The Forgotten Way* (Meditations), Ted Dekker, Copyright 2015
6. *The Forgotten Way* (Study Guide), Ted Decker, Copyright 2015
7. *Let Prayer Change Your Life Workbook*, Becky Tirabassi, Copyright 1995
8. *Emotionally Healthy Spirituality*, Peter Scazzero, Copyright 2006, 2017
9. *Emotionally Healthy Spirituality*, (Workbook), Peter & Geri Scazzsero, Copyright 2008, 2014, 2017
10. *Jesus>Religion*, Jefferson Bethke, Copyright 2013
11. *Illustrations Unlimited*, James S. Hewett, Copyright 1988
12. *Benedicte's Scrapbook*, William B. Gamb;e. Copyright 1954
13. *The Wounded Minister*, Guy Greenfield, Ph.D., Copyright 2001
14. *Streams in the Desert*, Mrs. Charles E. Cowman, Copyright 1925, 1953, 1965
15. *Tongues and Prophecy*, Stanley M. Horton, Copyright 1971-72
16. *You Can Be Emotionally Healed*, Dr. Morris Sheats, Copyright 1994
17. *The Complete Wineskin*, Harold R. Eberle, Copyright, 1993
18. *The New Strong's Complete Dictionary of Bible Words*, James Strong, LL.D., S.T.D., Copyright 1996
19. *Founder's Week Messages*, January31-February 6,1966, Moody Bible Institute, 820 North LaSalle Street, Chicago, Illinois 60610
20. *The Emmaus Code*, David Limbaugh, Copyright, 2015
21. *Word Meanings in the New Testament*, Ralph Earle, Copyright

1974, 1977, 1979, 1980, 1982, 1986

22. *Vine's Expository Dictionary of New Testament Words*, W. E Vines, M.A.

23. Love Thy *Neighbor . . .* , Aaron D. Davis, Copyright 2005

24. *Quantum Christianity*, Aaron D. Cavis, Copyright 2015

25. *Preparing to Receive the Baptism of the Holy Spirit*, Richard Heckman, Copyright, 1992

26. Finish *Strong*, Dan Green, Copyright, 2012, www.simpletruth.com

27. *The Koran Unveiled*, Charles S. Ruark, Jr., M.C., Copyright 2006

28. *Knight's Treasure of Illustrations*, Walter B. Knight, Copyright 1963

29. *Seeking Allah, Finding Jesus*, Nabeel Qureshi, Copyright 2014, 2016

30. *750 Engaging Illustrations*, Craig Brian Larson, Copyright 1998

31. *Unveiling ISLAM*, Ergun Mehmet Caner, Emir Fethi Canner, Copyright,2002, 2009

32. *Armageddon,* John F. Walvoord with Mark Hitchcock, Copyright 2007, www.tyndale.com

33. *Agents of Babylon*, Dr. David Jeremiah, Copyright 2015, www.tyn-dale.com

34. *YOU GOTTA KEEP DANCIN'*, Tim Hansel, Copyright 1985, David C. Cook

35. *Freedom Is a Choice*, Lawana Hughes, copyright 2014

36. No God But *One*, Nabeel Qureshi, Copyright 2016

37. *Learning to Love*, David Alsobrook, Copyright by David Alsobrook

38. *Churches that Abuse,* Ronald M. Enroth, Copyright 1992 by Ronald M. Enroth

39. *The Complete Word Study, Old Testament*, Copyright 1994, AMG INTERNATIONAL, INC.

40. *The Complete Word Study, New Testament*, Spiros Zodhiates Th.D., Copyright 1992

41. *Scars and Stripes*, Roy H. Cantrell, Copyright 2005

42. *Sow Joy: It's a Choice*, Roy H. Cantrell, Copyright 2013

43. *The Necessity of Prayer*, E.M. Bounds. Baker Books, Copyright 1991

44. *Corageous*, Dr. Robert Jeffress, Baker Books, Copyright 2020

About the Author

DR. ROY HAROLD CANTRELL was born in Shelby Gap, Kentucky, on August 22, 1939. He entered the ministry in 1959. Dr. Cantrell has a Doctor of Ministry degree from Christian Life School of Theology and a Doctor of Philosophy in Christian Counseling from Cornerstone University. He is a licensed pastoral counselor with the National Christian Counseling Association (NCCA), and he is board certified through NCCA as a substance abuse and addiction therapist, integrated marriage and family therapist, and temperament therapist.

Dr. Cantrell is the recently retired president and founder of City Gate Church, Chattanooga, TN, and served as senior pastor until his retirement in April 2012. Presently he serves as Pastor Emeritus with his son Dr. Roy H. (Howie) Cantrell president and founder of City Gate Church, Gallatin, TN. Additionally, while pastoring, Dr. Cantrell was the president and founder of Life Management Institute, a certified institute of the National Christian Counseling Association. He specialized in training counselors in the skill of temperament therapy, called Creation Therapy, and he assisted them in obtaining their faith-based licensure as well as various degrees. He is a trained Rule 31 court meditator in the state of Tennessee.

Dr. Cantrell is an author and occasionally speaks on the End Times. He answers some of the difficult questions people want to know about the End Times, including: "Is this present generation the first to see the end?" "Who will have the last word, the Church or Israel?" "Exploring the 'underworld' of Jerusalem." "Did God play a role in the recent disasters in America?" "How are Islam, religion, oil, and communism related to the End Times?" "What are the three keys to End Times living?"

Among his various life-long ministries include a twenty-five-year involvement as a certified teacher/trainer and associate clinical trainer with Evangelism Explosion, an international organization that teaches others to spread the salvation message and a love for missions. He has traveled extensively on international missions to Israel, Russia, England, Cyprus, Kenya, Africa, Guatemala, Mexico, Jamaica, Italy, France, Scotland, Canada, Honduras, and Cuba. He has studied Spanish at the *Centro Linguistico Maya* language school in Antigua, Guatemala, and is an Evangelism Explosion certified Spanish teacher/trainer.

Following is a list of his publications:

- *Thoughts with Meaning: Teaching Hints, Family Bible Reading, and Sentence Sermons for Teacher's Manual*
- *Keys to Camp Administration* – a manual for youth camp directors
- Numerous articles for his denomination's magazine
- Articles for *Halo Magazine*
- Article for *The Messenger*, a bimonthly publication of the National Christian Counselor's Association
- *Scars and Stripes: Hope for Adult Children of Alcoholic Families* – a book about his experiences growing up with an alcoholic father
- *Sow Joy: It's a Choice* – if not for hope the heart would break
- Devotions for his local church
- *Dancing on the Rubble: It's the Essence of Living*

Dr. Cantrell and his wife, Ina Kaye Goins Cantrell have been married for fifty-eight years and live in Cleveland, TN. They have two adult children, five grandchildren, and ten great-grandchildren.

CPSIA information can be obtained
at www.ICGtesting.com
Printed in the USA
LVHW012134020720
659546LV00005B/5

9 781977 211408